THE PLANT COOKBOOK FOR BEGINNERS

Your Essential Guide to Healthy and Delicious Vegan Meals.
100 Easy and Healthy Recipes You'll Want to Make All the Time

Alyssa Adler

TABLE OF CONTENTS

INTRODUCTION

In recent years, there has been a growing interest in plant-based diets as an alternative to traditional meat-based diets. With concerns about health, animal welfare, and the environment on the rise, more and more people are turning to plant-based foods as a way to improve their well-being and reduce their impact on the planet.

If you're considering making the switch to a plant-based diet, you're not alone. Research has shown that a plant-based diet can improve heart health, lower the risk of type 2 diabetes, and even help with weight management. Additionally, adopting a plant-based diet can reduce the carbon footprint of food production, since raising animals for food requires more resources and produces more greenhouse gases than growing crops.

But for many people, the idea of giving up meat, dairy, and eggs can be daunting. That's where this plant-based cookbook comes in. We believe that plant-based food doesn't have to be bland or boring - in fact, it can be vibrant, delicious, and exciting. Our cookbook is designed to help you discover the joy and creativity of plant-based cooking, whether you're a seasoned vegan or just starting to explore plant-based options.

Inside this cookbook, you'll find a variety of easy-to-follow recipes that are bursting with flavor and nutrition. From hearty main courses to satisfying snacks and desserts, our recipes are designed to be both delicious and nutritious, so you can feel good about what you eat.

So if you're looking to try something new, improve your health, or reduce your carbon footprint, we invite you to join us on a culinary journey that celebrates the beauty and diversity of plant-based food. Whether you're a seasoned plant-based eater or just starting out, we're confident that this cookbook will inspire you to create delicious, flavorful, and nourishing meals that will leave you feeling both satisfied and energized.

CHAPTER 1 : BREAKFAST

VEGAN BANANA PANCAKES

Fluffy and moist banana pancakes made with simple ingredients make an easy and delicious breakfast treat.

- Prep Time: 10 minutes
- Cook Time: 15 minutes
- Total Time: 25 minutes
- Servings: 4

Ingredients:

- 2 ripe bananas
- 2 cups of flour
- 1 tablespoon of baking powder
- 1/4 teaspoon of salt
- 2 cups of unsweetened almond milk
- 2 tablespoons of maple syrup
- 1 teaspoon vanilla extract
- 1 tablespoon of coconut oil

Directions:

1. Begin by mashing the ripe bananas until smooth in a bowl.
2. To make the banana mixture, mix the mashed bananas with flour, baking powder, and salt in a bowl until well combined.
3. Pour in the almond milk, maple syrup, vanilla extract, and mix the ingredients until thoroughly combined and form a smooth batter.
4. Heat a non-stick pan and pour one tablespoon of coconut oil to cover the surface of the pan evenly.
5. Put a quarter cup of the batter onto the heated pan and cook each side for about 2 to 3 minutes, or until it achieves a light brown color.
6. Remove from the heat when finished and repeat the process until all the batter is used.
7. Serve immediately and enjoy!

Nutritional breakdown per serving:

Calories: 355 kcal, Protein: 8 grams, Carbohydrates: 68 grams, Fat: 7 grams, Saturated Fat: 4 grams, Sodium: 57 milligrams, Fiber: 4 grams, and Sugar: 13 grams.

TOFU SCRAMBLE

A protein-packed vegan alternative to scrambled eggs, tofu scramble is a great start to the day, seasoned with your favorite spices and herbs.

- Prep Time: 10 minutes
- Cook Time: 15 minutes
- Total Time: 25 minutes
- Servings: 4

Ingredients:

- 1 block (14 oz) of firm tofu
- 1 tablespoon of olive oil
- 1/2 onion, diced
- 1/2 red bell pepper, diced
- 3 cloves of garlic, minced
- 1/2 teaspoon of paprika
- 1/2 teaspoon of turmeric
- 1/2 teaspoon of cumin
- 1/4 teaspoon of salt
- 1/4 teaspoon of black pepper
- 2 tablespoons of nutritional yeast (optional)

Directions:

1. To eliminate excess water, drain and press the tofu for approximately 10 minutes.
2. Crumble the tofu in a bowl and set aside.
3. Begin by heating olive oil in a big pan over medium heat, and sauté onion and red bell pepper until they soften, which typically takes about 5 minutes.
4. Add garlic, paprika, turmeric, cumin, salt, and black pepper then cook for another 2 minutes.
5. Add crumbled tofu and stir well to combine with the spices and vegetables. Cook for an additional 5-7 minutes or until the tofu is heated through and slightly browned.
6. Take the pan off the heat and, if desired, add nutritional yeast for a cheese-like taste.
7. Serve hot with your favorite toppings like avocado, salsa, and fresh herbs.

Nutritional Information per serving:

Calories: 120kcal Total Fat: 7g Saturated Fat: 1g Sodium: 168mg Total Carbohydrates: 5g Fiber: 1g Sugar: 1g Protein: 10g

Nutritional breakdown per serving:

Calories: 120 kcal, Protein: 10 grams, Carbohydrates: 5 grams, Fat: 7 grams, Saturated Fat: 1 grams, Sodium: 168 milligrams, Fiber: 1 grams, and Sugar: 1 grams.

CHIA PUDDING

This creamy, delicious, and nutrient-rich breakfast dish can be prepared in advance for busy mornings.

- Prep Time: 5-10 minutes
- Total Time: 2-3 hours or overnight
- Servings: 2

Ingredients:

- 1/4 cup of chia seeds
- 1 cup of unsweetened almond milk
- 1 tablespoon of maple syrup (optional)
- 1/2 teaspoon of vanilla extract (optional)
- Fruits, nuts, and seeds for topping (optional)

Directions:

1. In a small bowl or jar, stir together chia seeds and almond milk.
2. Whisk the mixture vigorously to prevent clumping.
3. Add maple syrup and vanilla extract until combined (optional).
4. Cover and refrigerate the pudding for at least 2-3 hours or overnight.
5. Stir the pudding well before serving and add your desired toppings like fruits, nuts, or seeds.

Nutritional breakdown per serving: Calories:

120 kcal, Protein: 5 grams, Carbohydrates: 9 grams, Fat: 7 grams, Saturated Fat: 1 grams, Sodium: 160 milligrams, Fiber: 8 grams, and Sugar: 1 grams.

QUINOA SALAD

This easy-to-make quinoa salad is filled with colorful veggies, and it can be prepared in advance for a quick and healthy meal during the week.

- Prep Time: 20 minutes
- Cook Time: 20-25 minutes
- Total Time: 40-45 minutes
- Servings: 4-6

Ingredients:

- 1 cup of quinoa
- 2 cups of water
- 2 tablespoons of olive oil
- 1/4 cup of lemon juice
- 1/2 teaspoon of salt
- 1/4 teaspoon of black pepper
- 1 can of chickpeas, drained and rinsed
- 1/2 cup of chopped fresh parsley
- 1/4 cup of chopped fresh mint
- 1/2 cup of chopped cucumber
- 1/2 cup of cherry tomatoes, halved
- 1/4 cup of chopped red onion

Directions:

1. Rinse the quinoa under running water, then cook in a pot with 2 cups of water according to package instructions (usually takes 20-25 minutes).
2. When the quinoa is done cooking, use a fork to fluff it up, and then allow it to cool by setting it aside.
3. In a large bowl, whisk together olive oil, lemon juice, salt, and black pepper to make the dressing.
4. To prepare the dressing, combine olive oil, lemon juice, salt, and black pepper in a sizeable bowl, and whisk thoroughly until well-mixed.
5. Add in the cooled quinoa to the bowl and toss everything together until well combined.
6. After covering the bowl with plastic wrap, let the quinoa salad cool in the fridge for at least 30 minutes.
7. Stir well and serve cold on its own or with additional greens, and enjoy.

Nutritional breakdown per serving (based on 4 servings):

Calories: 29 kcal, Protein: 11 grams, Carbohydrates: 44 grams, Fat: 10 grams, Saturated Fat: 1 grams, Sodium: 312 milligrams, Fiber: 11 grams, and Sugar: 5 grams.

VEGAN FRIED RICE

This flavorful fried rice, packed with veggies and protein, can be made in large batches and eaten throughout the week.

- Prep Time: 15 minutes
- Cook Time: 25 minutes
- Total Time: 40 minutes
- Servings: 4-6

Ingredients:

- 2 cups of cooked and chilled brown rice
- 1 tablespoon of vegetable oil
- 1/2 onion, diced
- 2 cloves of garlic, minced
- 1/2 cup of green peas
- 1/2 cup of sliced carrots
- 1/2 cup of sliced mushrooms
- 1/2 cup diced red bell pepper
- 1/4 cup soy sauce or tamari
- 1 tablespoon of sesame oil (optional)
- 1/4 teaspoon of black pepper
- Optional topping: sliced green onions and sesame seeds

Directions:

1. To begin the preparation of the ingredients, heat the vegetable oil in a large skillet or wok on medium-high heat.
2. Add onion and garlic then stir-fry for 2-3 minutes until fragrant.
3. Add green peas, carrots, mushrooms, and red bell pepper into the wok. Stir-fry for an additional 3-4 minutes until the vegetables are tender.
4. Add chilled brown rice into the wok and toss everything together until well combined.
5. Add soy sauce or tamari, sesame oil (optional), and black pepper to the wok. Keep stirring until everything is heated through and well coated with the sauce for about 3-5 minutes.
6. Remove the wok from heat and sprinkle with sliced green onions and sesame seeds (optional) for garnish.
7. Serve hot and enjoy.

Nutritional breakdown per serving (based on 4 servings):

Calories: 238 kcal, Protein: 6 grams, Carbohydrates: 40 grams, Fat: 6 grams, Saturated Fat: 1 grams, Sodium: 580 milligrams, Fiber: 6 grams, and Sugar: 6 grams.

CARROT AND GINGER SOUP

Make a big batch of this piping hot soup to warm up your week. It's quick to make, filling, and packed with nutrients.

- Prep Time: 25 minutes
- Cook Time: 40 minutes
- Total Time: 1 hour 5 minutes
- Servings: 4

Ingredients:

- 2 tablespoons of olive oil
- 1 onion, chopped
- 2 cloves of garlic, minced
- 1 tablespoon of grated ginger
- 1 lb (450g) of carrots, peeled and chopped
- 4 cups (950ml) of vegetable broth
- Salt and black pepper, to taste
- Optional toppings: Plain Greek yogurt, chopped fresh parsley, and croutons

Directions:

1. Heat the olive oil in a large pot over medium-high heat until it has reached the optimal temperature for cooking purposes.
2. Add onion and garlic and stir-fry for 2-3 minutes until fragrant.
3. Add grated ginger and chopped carrots into the pot and stir everything together.
4. Add a quantity of vegetable broth to your pot and heat it up until it starts boiling.
5. Reduce heat to low and let it simmer for 35-40 minutes until the carrots are very soft and tender.
6. To achieve a smooth consistency, you have the option of using an immersion blender or transferring the soup to a blender for pureeing.
7. Return the soup to the pot and reheat over low heat.
8. To suit your taste, feel free to add salt and black pepper to the soup in the amount that you prefer.
9. Serve the soup in bowls and, if desired, top off with plain Greek yogurt, chopped fresh parsley, and croutons for garnishing.
10. Serve hot and enjoy.

Nutritional breakdown per serving:

Calories: 150 kcal, Protein: 3 grams, Carbohydrates: 21 grams, Fat: 7 grams, Saturated Fat: 1 grams, Sodium: 850 milligrams, Fiber: 5 grams, and Sugar: 10 grams.

OVERNIGHT OATS

Oatmeal is a classic breakfast food, and this tasty variation can be prepared the night before and refrigerated for easy mornings.

- Prep Time: 5-10 minutes
- Cook Time: 0 minutes
- Total Time: 5-10 minutes (plus overnight chill time)
- Servings: 1

Ingredients:

- 1/2 cup of rolled oats
- 1/2 cup of unsweetened almond milk
- 1/2 banana, mashed (or 1 tablespoon of maple syrup)
- 1/2 teaspoon of vanilla extract (optional)
- Pinch of salt
- Toppings such as fruit, nuts, or seeds (optional)

Directions:

1. In a container with a lid or a mason jar, mix together rolled oats, unsweetened almond milk, mashed banana (or maple syrup), vanilla extract (if using), and a pinch of salt.
2. Close the container tightly and give it a good shake to combine all ingredients.
3. Refrigerate the container overnight (or at least 2 hours) to allow the oats to soften and flavors to meld.
4. In the morning, give the container a good stir and add desired toppings like fresh or dried fruits, nuts, or seeds.
5. Enjoy your quick and easy, no-cook breakfast!

Nutritional breakdown per serving:

Calories: 270 kcal, Protein: 8 grams, Carbohydrates: 50 grams, Fat: 5 grams, Saturated Fat: 1 grams, Sodium: 170 milligrams, Fiber: 8 grams, and Sugar: 10 grams.

AVOCADO TOAST

A fan favorite for breakfast, this plant-based version of avocado toast is loaded with vitamins and fiber.

- Prep Time: 5 minutes
- Cook Time: 5 minutes
- Total Time: 10 minutes
- Servings: 2

Ingredients:

- 2 slices of whole grain bread
- 1 ripe avocado
- 1 garlic clove, minced
- 1 small tomato, sliced
- 1/4 teaspoon red pepper flakes (optional)
- Salt and black pepper
- 2 eggs (optional)

Directions:

1. Begin by setting the oven temperature at 350°F (175°C) and wait for it to completely preheat before starting your cooking.
2. Gently toast the bread slices using a toaster or broiler until they turn crisp.
3. Cut the avocado lengthwise and carefully take out the seed. Use a spoon to extract the avocado meat into a bowl, then mash it with a fork to create a smooth consistency.
4. Stir in minced garlic, red pepper flakes (if using), and a pinch of salt and black pepper to the mashed avocado.
5. Spread the mashed avocado evenly onto each slice of toasted bread.
6. Add sliced tomatoes on top of the avocado mash.
7. When making eggs, warm up a non-stick frying pan over medium heat and crack the eggs right into it. Cook until the desired level of doneness is reached.
8. Place the cooked eggs on top of the avocado toast.
9. Sprinkle with additional red pepper flakes (optional) and serve immediately.

Nutritional breakdown per serving:

Calories (based on 2 servings): 232 kcal, Protein: 10 grams, Carbohydrates: 19 grams, Fat: 15 grams, Saturated Fat: 3 grams, Sodium: 346 milligrams, Fiber: 8 grams, and Sugar: 2 grams.

VEGAN BREAKFAST BURRITO

Filled with spiced sweet potato, black beans, avocado and topped with salsa, this breakfast burrito is easy, filling and satisfying.

- Prep Time: 10 minutes
- Cook Time: 10 minutes
- Total Time: 20 minutes
- Servings: 4

Ingredients:

- 1 tablespoon of olive oil
- 1/2 onion, diced
- 1/2 red bell pepper, diced
- 1/2 green bell pepper, diced
- 1 cup of diced potatoes
- 1/4 teaspoon of garlic powder
- Salt and black pepper
- 4 large flour tortillas
- 1 avocado, sliced
- 1/2 cup of canned black beans that have been drained and rinsed well
- 1/2 cup of either Pico de Gallo or salsa
- 1/4 cup of chopped fresh cilantro
- Hot sauce (optional)

Directions:

1. Heat up some olive oil in a large skillet over medium-high heat. Proceed to sauté onions and bell peppers until they are soft.
2. Add diced potatoes and garlic powder to the skillet, sprinkle with salt and black pepper. Cook your food for roughly 10 to 12 minutes, or until the potatoes become tender and acquire a light brown color.
3. Warm the tortillas in the microwave or on a skillet.
4. To assemble each burrito, divide the potato mixture among the tortillas.
5. Add sliced avocado, black beans, Pico de Gallo (or salsa), and chopped fresh cilantro.
6. Drizzle with hot sauce (optional) as desired.
7. Roll up the burrito tightly and cut in half before serving.
8. Enjoy your delicious and satisfying Vegan Breakfast Burritos!

Nutritional breakdown per serving (based on 4 servings):

Calories: 329 kcal, Protein: 9 grams, Carbohydrates: 45 grams, Fat: 13 grams, Saturated Fat: 2 grams, Sodium: 479 milligrams, Fiber: 9 grams, and Sugar: 4 grams.

TOFU AND VEGGIE STIR FRY

This stir fry is easy, quick, and tasty. Make a big batch on Sunday for a week's worth of healthy and flavorful meals to keep you energized.

- Prep Time: 15 minutes
- Cook Time: 20 minutes
- Total Time: 35 minutes
- Servings: 4

Ingredients:

- 1 tablespoon of vegetable oil
- Cube and drain 14 oz. of firm tofu
- Salt and black pepper
- 1 onion, sliced
- 2 carrots, peeled and sliced
- 2 bell peppers, sliced
- 2 cups of broccoli florets
- 1 tablespoon of minced garlic
- 1 tablespoon of grated ginger
- 1 tablespoon of cornstarch
- 1/4 cup of soy sauce
- 1/4 cup of vegetable broth
- 1 tablespoon of honey
- 1 teaspoon of sesame oil (optional)
- 2 green onions, sliced
- Sesame seeds (optional)

Directions:

1. Using a large skillet or wok, heat up some vegetable oil over medium-high heat, then add in the cubed tofu. Season it with salt and black pepper, then cook until it becomes crispy and acquires a light brown color. After that, remove the tofu from the skillet and set it aside.
2. In the same skillet, add sliced onion, carrots, bell peppers, broccoli florets, minced garlic, and grated ginger. Cook until the veggies turn tender, which typically takes around 10-12 minutes.
3. In a small bowl, whisk cornstarch, soy sauce, vegetable broth, honey, and sesame oil (if using) together.

4. Pour the sauce all over the vegetables, then stir them well until the sauce covers them evenly. Heat the mixture for roughly 2 to 3 minutes, or until the sauce thickens to the consistency you prefer.
5. Add the cooked tofu back into the skillet and stir everything together. Cook another 1-2 minutes to heat up the tofu.
6. When ready, take the mixture off the heat and embellish it with sliced green onions and sesame seeds, if preferred.
7. Serve the Tofu and Veggie Stir Fry over rice or noodles, if desired.

Nutritional breakdown per serving (based on 4 servings):

Calories: 235 kcal, Protein: 18 grams, Carbohydrates: 20 grams, Fat: 11 grams, Saturated Fat: 1 grams, Sodium: 871 milligrams, Fiber: 20 grams, and Sugar: 9 grams.

VEGAN BISCUITS AND GRAVY

Crumbly, buttery, and savory vegan biscuits smothered in creamy gravy make for a decadent and hearty breakfast.

- Prep Time: 10 minutes
- Cook Time: 20 minutes
- Total Time: 30 minutes
- Servings: 4

Ingredients:

For the biscuits:

- 2 cups of all-purpose flour
- 1 tablespoon of baking powder
- 1/2 teaspoon of baking soda
- 1/2 teaspoon of salt
- 6 tablespoons of vegan butter, chilled
- 3/4 cup of non-dairy milk
- 1 tablespoon of apple cider vinegar

For the gravy:

- 1/4 cup of vegan butter
- 1/4 cup of all-purpose flour
- 2 cups of non-dairy milk
- Salt and black pepper
- 1/2 teaspoon of garlic powder
- 1/2 teaspoon of onion powder

Directions:

1. Preheat the oven to 450°F.
2. Whisk all-purpose flour, baking powder, baking soda, and salt together in a large mixing bowl until fully combined.
3. Cut chilled vegan butter into the dry ingredients until the mixture resembles coarse crumbs.
4. Mix non-dairy milk and apple cider vinegar in a small bowl, stirring until fully combined.

5. Add the non-dairy milk mixture to the dry ingredients and mix until just combined. Do not overmix.
6. Place the dough on a floured surface and pat it out to 1 inch thickness. Slice the biscuits by using a glass or a biscuit cutter.
7. Put the biscuits onto a baking sheet that has been covered with a parchment paper. Bake the biscuits for 10-12 minutes or until they acquire a pleasing golden-brown color.

For the gravy:

1. Using a large skillet, melt the vegan butter by applying medium heat.
2. Add all-purpose flour and whisk until smooth.
3. Add non-dairy milk to the mixture slowly and keep whisking continuously until it thickens and begins to simmer.
4. Incorporate the garlic powder, onion powder, salt, and black pepper to your taste, and stir them thoroughly into the mixture.
5. Reduce the heat and continue to cook the gravy for 2-3 more minutes, stirring constantly.

To serve:

1. Lower the heat and keep stirring the gravy constantly while cooking it for an additional 2-3 minutes.
2. Spoon the gravy over the biscuits.
3. Serve hot.

Nutritional breakdown per serving (based on 4 servings):

Calories: 438 kcal, Carbohydrates: 8 grams, Fat: 25 grams, Saturated Fat: 8 grams, Sodium: 804 milligrams, Fiber: 2 grams.

VEGAN PROTEIN SMOOTHIE BOWL

This protein-packed smoothie bowl incorporates fruits, vegetables, and plant-based proteins for a delicious and nutritious breakfast.

- Prep Time: 5 minutes
- Cook Time: 0 minutes
- Total Time: 5 minutes
- Servings: 1

Ingredients:

- 1 ripe banana, frozen
- 1/2 cup frozen mixed berries
- 1 scoop plant-based protein powder
- 1/4 cup non-dairy milk
- 1/4 cup water
- Select your favorite toppings like fruit, granola, nuts, or seeds.

Directions:

1. Add frozen banana, frozen mixed berries, plant-based protein powder, non-dairy milk, and water to a blender.
2. Blend until smooth and creamy, using tamper/scraping as needed.
3. Pour the smoothie into a bowl.
4. Incorporate the toppings you prefer, such as sliced fruit, granola, nuts, or seeds.

Nutritional breakdown per serving:

Calories: 345 kcal, Protein: 20 grams, Carbohydrates: 60 grams, Fat: 3 grams, Saturated Fat: 1 grams, Sodium: 265 milligrams, Fiber: 10 grams, and Sugar: 31 grams.

VEGAN VEGGIE BURGER

These hearty burgers made with beans, grains, and vegetables

- Prep Time: 20 minutes
- Cook Time: 10 minutes
- Total Time: 30 minutes
- Servings: 4

Ingredients:

- 15 oz black beans, drained and rinsed
- 1/2 cup of cooked brown rice
- 1/2 cup of finely chopped mushrooms
- 1/4 cup of finely chopped onion
- 1/4 cup finely chopped bell pepper
- 2 cloves of garlic, minced
- 2 tablespoons of ketchup
- 1 teaspoon of smoked paprika
- 1/2 teaspoon of cumin
- 1/4 teaspoon of salt
- 1/4 teaspoon of black pepper
- 1/4 cup of breadcrumbs
- 1 tablespoon of olive oil

For serving:

- 4 hamburger buns
- Lettuce, tomato, onion, and condiments of your choice

Directions:

1. Mash the black beans using a fork or potato masher in a large bowl until they become smooth, but with some texture remaining.
2. Add cooked brown rice, chopped mushrooms, onion, bell pepper, garlic, ketchup, smoked paprika, cumin, salt, and black pepper. Mix well.
3. Add breadcrumbs and mix until well-combined.
4. Separate the mixture into four portions of the same size and shape each part into a patty for the burgers.
5. Heat up the non-stick skillet over a medium-high heat, then add the olive oil to warm it up.

6. Add burger patties to the skillet and cook for 4-5 minutes on each side or until browned and heated through.

To serve:

1. Toast hamburger buns, if desired.
2. For each bun, position one patty on the bottom half.
3. Add lettuce, tomato, onion, and condiments of your choice.
4. Top each burger with the top half of the bun.
5. Serve hot.

Nutritional breakdown per serving:

Calories: 321 kcal, Protein: 16 grams, Carbohydrates: 52 grams, Fat: 7 grams, Saturated Fat: 1 grams, Sodium: 525 milligrams, Fiber: 12 grams, and Sugar: 6 grams.

VEGAN STUFFED PEPPERS

Filled with a mixture of lentils, rice, and veggies, these stuffed peppers are a delicious and easy-to-prep meal for the week.

- Prep Time: 20 minutes
- Cook Time: 45 minutes
- Total Time: 1 hour 5 minutes
- Servings: 4

Ingredients:

- 4 large bell peppers, tops and seeds removed
- 1 cup of cooked brown rice
- 15 oz can of black beans, drained
- 1 can (14.5 oz) of diced tomatoes, drained
- 1/2 cup of frozen corn
- 1/4 cup of chopped onion
- 1/4 cup of chopped cilantro
- 1 tablespoon of chili powder
- 1 teaspoon of cumin
- 1/2 teaspoon of salt
- 1/4 teaspoon of black pepper
- 1/2 cup of shredded vegan cheese

Directions:

1. Set oven to 375°F (190°C).
2. In a large bowl, mix together cooked brown rice, black beans, diced tomatoes, frozen corn, chopped onion, chopped cilantro, chili powder, cumin, salt, and black pepper.
3. Stuff each bell pepper with the rice and bean mixture.
4. Place stuffed peppers in a baking dish.
5. Cover the dish with foil.
6. Bake for 40 minutes.
7. Remove the foil and sprinkle shredded vegan cheese on top of the peppers.
8. Bake uncovered for another 5-10 minutes or until cheese is melted and bubbly.

Nutritional breakdown per serving: Calories:

277 kcal, Protein: 15 grams, Carbohydrates: 42 grams, Fat: 7 grams, Saturated Fat: 2 grams, Sodium: 588 milligrams, Fiber: 12 grams, and Sugar: 10 grams.

VEGAN FRENCH TOAST

Thick slices of bread are coated in a sweet batter made with non-dairy milk, cinnamon, and vanilla, then pan-fried to create a delicious and fulfilling vegan breakfast.

- Prep Time: 10 minutes
- Cook Time: 15 minutes
- Total Time: 25 minutes
- Servings: 4

Ingredients:

- 1/2 cup of chickpea flour
- 1 tablespoon of nutritional yeast
- 1/2 teaspoon of ground cinnamon
- 1/4 teaspoon of ground nutmeg
- 1 cup of non-dairy milk
- 1 tablespoon of maple syrup
- 1 teaspoon of vanilla extract
- 8 slices of bread
- Vegan butter or oil, for frying

Directions:

1. In a shallow dish, whisk together chickpea flour, nutritional yeast, cinnamon, and nutmeg.
2. Add non-dairy milk, maple syrup, and vanilla extract. Whisk until smooth.
3. Melt vegan butter or heat oil in a large non-stick skillet over medium heat.
4. Dip each slice of bread in the chickpea flour mixture, making sure it's evenly coated on both sides.
5. Cook each bread slice over medium heat for 2-3 minutes per side, or until they turn golden brown.
6. Enjoy while still hot and top with your preferred toppings, such as fresh fruit slices, whipped cream alternative, or maple syrup.

Nutritional breakdown per serving: Calories:

272 kcal, Protein: 8 grams, Carbohydrates: 43 grams, Fat: 6 grams, Saturated Fat: 1 grams, Sodium: 407 milligrams, Fiber: 5 grams, and Sugar: 8 grams.

VEGAN STRAWBERRY AND BANANA SMOOTHIE BOWL

This vegan strawberry and banana smoothie bowl is a delicious and healthy breakfast or snack choice. Made with just a few wholesome ingredients and topped with your favorite toppings, this smoothie bowl is customizable and easy to make.

- Preparation Time: 10 minutes
- Total Time: 10 minutes
- Servings: 2

Ingredients:

- 200g frozen banana chunks
- 150g frozen strawberries
- 1/2 cup unsweetened almond milk
- 1 tbsp maple syrup
- 1/2 tsp vanilla extract
- Fresh fruit 1, nuts, seeds, and coconut flakes for topping

Directions:

1. Combine the frozen strawberries, frozen bananas, unsweetened almond milk, maple syrup, and vanilla extract in the blender carafe. Process the mixture until it reaches a smooth and velvety consistency.
2. Pour the smoothie mixture into a bowl.
3. Add your desired toppings, such as fresh fruit, nuts, seeds, and coconut flakes.
4. Serve and enjoy!

Nutritional breakdown per serving: Calories:

143 kcal, Protein: 2 grams, Carbohydrates: 34 grams, Fat: 2 grams, Saturated Fat: 1 grams, Sodium: 0 milligrams, Fiber: 5 grams, and Sugar: 19 grams.

OATMEAL PANCAKES

Fluffy and delicious pancakes made with oats, almond milk, and cinnamon for a hearty and healthy breakfast.

- Prep Time: 5 minutes Cook
- Time: 10 minutes
- Total Time: 15 minutes
- Servings: 2-3 (6-9 pancakes)

Ingredients:

- 1 cup of quick oats
- 1 cup of non-dairy milk
- 1 ripe banana
- 1 teaspoon of baking powder
- 1/2 teaspoon of ground cinnamon
- 1/4 teaspoon of salt
- 1/2 teaspoon of vanilla extract
- Vegan butter or oil, for frying
- Optional toppings: fresh fruit, maple syrup, vegan whipped cream

Directions:

1. Combine quick oats, non-dairy milk, ripe banana, baking powder, ground cinnamon, salt, and vanilla extract in a blender or food processor and blend until the mixture becomes smooth.
2. Melt vegan butter or heat oil in a non-stick skillet over medium heat.
3. Take a measuring cup that holds a quarter cup of batter, and use it to pour the batter onto the skillet.
4. Cook for 2-3 minutes on each side, or until golden brown.
5. Repeat with remaining batter.
6. Serve hot with your favorite toppings.

Nutritional breakdown per serving (3 pancakes):

Calories: 250 kcal, Protein: 7 grams, Carbohydrates: 44 grams, Fat: 6 grams, Saturated Fat: 1 grams, Sodium: 310 milligrams, Fiber: 6 grams, and Sugar: 11 grams.

VEGAN BREAKFAST SANDWICH

This plant-based sandwich is made with tofu, vegan cheese, and veggies, all served on an English muffin for a delicious and filling breakfast.

- Prep Time: 10 minutes
- Cook Time: 10 minutes
- Total Time: 20 minutes
- Servings: 1

Ingredients:

- 1 English muffin, halved
- 1/4 cup of vegan mayonnaise
- 1/2 tablespoon of dijon mustard
- 1/2 teaspoon of agave nectar
- Pinch of salt and pepper
- 1/4 block of firm tofu, sliced
- Vegan cheese slices
- Vegan bacon slices
- 1/4 avocado, sliced
- Handful of baby spinach

Directions:

1. In a small bowl, mix vegan mayonnaise, dijon mustard, agave nectar, salt, and pepper until a sauce is formed.
2. Toast the English muffin halves and set aside.
3. Using a non-stick skillet, set the heat to medium and heat it up. Then, cook both sides of the tofu slices until they turn lightly brown.
4. Add vegan cheese slices on top of the tofu to melt.
5. Cook the vegan bacon slices according to package instructions.
6. Assemble the sandwich by spreading the sauce on the toasted English muffin halves.
7. Top with cooked tofu with melted vegan cheese, vegan bacon slices, avocado slices, and baby spinach.
8. Serve hot.

Nutritional breakdown per serving: Calories:

488 kcal, Protein: 18 grams, Carbohydrates: 42 grams, Fat: 29 grams, Saturated Fat: 8 grams, Sodium: 1048 milligrams, Fiber: 11 grams, and Sugar: 6 grams.

VEGAN QUINOA STEW

A flavorful and hearty stew made with quinoa, sweet potatoes, chickpeas, and spices, perfect for meal prep lunches or dinners.

- Prep Time: 15 minutes
- Cook Time: 45 minutes
- Total Time: 1 hour
- Servings: 4-6

Ingredients:

- 1 tablespoon of olive oil
- 1 onion, chopped
- 4 cloves of garlic, minced
- 2 teaspoons of ground cumin
- 1 teaspoon of smoked paprika
- 1/2 teaspoon of ground turmeric
- 1/2 teaspoon of salt
- 2 cups of vegetable broth
- One 14.5-ounce can of drained diced tomatoes
- 1 can (15 oz) black beans, drained
- 1 cup of uncooked quinoa, rinsed
- 2 cups of chopped sweet potatoes
- 2 cups of chopped kale
- 1 tablespoon of lemon juice

Directions:

1. In a big pot, warm up the olive oil using medium heat.
2. Include onion and sauté until it turns translucent, which takes approximately 5 minutes.
3. Stir in garlic, cumin, paprika, turmeric, and salt and cook for another minute.
4. Pour in vegetable broth, diced tomatoes, black beans, quinoa, and sweet potatoes and bring to a boil.
5. Bring down the heat to the minimum level, and cover the pot to allow the mixture to simmer for approximately 30-35 minutes until the sweet potatoes and quinoa are cooked all the way through.
6. Add the chopped kale to the mixture and stir well, then continue cooking for an additional 3-5 minutes until the kale has become wilted.

7. Stir in lemon juice.
8. Stir in lemon juice.
9. Serve hot.

Nutritional breakdown per serving:

Calories: 389 kcal, Protein: 17 grams, Carbohydrates: 69 grams, Fat: 87 grams, Saturated Fat: 1 grams, Sodium: 890 milligrams, Fiber: 115 grams, and Sugar: 9 grams.

VEGAN GREEK YOGURT PARFAIT

A simple and delicious breakfast parfait made with plant-based Greek yogurt, fresh fruit, and granola for a healthy and tasty morning meal.

- Prep Time: 5 minutes
- Total Time: 5 minutes
- Servings: 1

Ingredients:

- 1 cup of dairy-free Greek-style yogurt
- 1/2 cup of mixed berries
- 1/4 cup of granola
- 1 tablespoon of maple syrup

Directions:

1. In a small bowl or glass, layer the dairy-free Greek-style yogurt, mixed berries, and granola.
2. Drizzle maple syrup on top.
3. Serve immediately.

Nutritional breakdown per serving:

Calories: 319 kcal, Protein: 14 grams, Carbohydrates: 51 grams, Fat: 8 grams, Saturated Fat: 1 grams, Sodium: 87 milligrams, Fiber: 7 grams, and Sugar: 26 grams.

CHAPTER 2 :
LUNCH

VEGAN LENTIL SOUP

A hearty and warming soup made with lentils and vegetables.

- Prep Time: 15 minutes
- Cook Time: 1 hour 15 minutes
- Total Time: 1 hour 30 minutes
- Servings: 6-8

Ingredients:

- 1 tablespoon of olive oil
- 1 onion, chopped
- 2 carrots, chopped
- 2 celery stalks, chopped
- 4 cloves of garlic, minced
- 1 teaspoon of ground cumin
- 1 teaspoon of smoked paprika
- 1/2 teaspoon of dried thyme
- 1/2 teaspoon of salt
- 1/4 teaspoon of black pepper
- 6 cups of vegetable broth
- 2 cups of split red lentils, rinsed
- 14.5 oz diced tomatoes with juice
- 1/4 cup of chopped fresh parsley
- Lemon wedges for serving

Directions:

1. Using a larger pot, heat the olive oil over medium heat.
2. Cook the onion, carrots, and celery for around 5 minutes until the onion turns translucent.
3. Add garlic, cumin, smoked paprika, thyme, salt, and black pepper to the mixture and cook for another minute while stirring.
4. Pour in vegetable broth and split red lentils and bring to a boil.
5. Turn down the heat to low, place a cover on the pot, and let it simmer for about one hour or until the lentils are tender.
6. Stir in diced tomatoes and fresh parsley and let cook for another 5 minutes.
7. Serve hot with lemon wedges.

Nutritional breakdown per serving (based on 6 servings):

Calories: 251 kcal, Protein: 15 grams, Carbohydrates: 42 grams, Fat: 4 grams, Saturated Fat: 1 grams, Cholesterol: 0 milligrams, Sodium: 1282 milligrams, Fiber: 16 grams, and Sugar: 6 grams.

VEGAN CAESAR SALAD WITH CHICKPEA CROUTONS

Transform the traditional Caesar salad into a delectable and healthy vegan version with chickpea croutons. This salad boasts crunchy and protein-rich chickpea croutons, accompanied by a luscious and dairy-free Caesar dressing. Feel free to whip this up as a light and nutritious lunch or dinner option.

- Preparation Time: 15 minutes
- Cooking Time: 30 minutes
- Total Time: 45 minutes
- Servings: 4

Ingredients:

For the Chickpea Croutons:

- 1 can of chickpeas (400g), drained and rinsed
- 1 tbsp olive oil
- 1 tsp garlic powder
- 1/2 tsp smoked paprika
- 1/2 tsp sea salt

For the Dressing:

- Soak 1/2 cup of cashews in boiling water for 15 minutes
- 1/4 cup water
- 1 clove garlic, minced
- 1 tsp dijon mustard
- 1 tbsp nutritional yeast
- 1 tbsp fresh lemon juice
- 1/2 tsp sea salt

For the Salad:

- 2 chop and wash large romaine lettuce heads
- 1/4 cup vegan parmesan cheese
- 1/4 cup fresh parsley leaves

Directions:

1. Preheat the oven to 400°F.
2. In a mixing bowl, blend together the chickpeas, smoked paprika, garlic powder, sea salt and olive oil until thoroughly combined.
3. Begin by covering a baking sheet with parchment paper. Then, spread the chickpeas out evenly on the sheet. Bake the chickpeas in the oven at 375°F for 25-30 minutes until they turn a crispy, golden brown color.
4. While the chickpeas are cooking, make the dressing. Drain and rinse the soaked cashews and combine them in a blender with water, garlic, dijon mustard, nutritional yeast, fresh lemon juice, and sea salt. Blend until smooth and creamy.
5. Put together the salad by adding chopped romaine lettuce, vegan parmesan cheese, and fresh parsley leaves into a large mixing bowl. Mix all of the ingredients thoroughly.
6. Drizzle the cashew dressing over the salad and toss until the lettuce is evenly coated.
7. Serve the salad in individual bowls and top with the crispy chickpea croutons. Enjoy!

Nutritional breakdown per serving:

Calories: 244 kcal, Protein: 10 grams, Carbohydrates: 27 grams, Fat: 13 grams, Saturated Fat: 7 grams, Sodium: 27 milligrams, Fiber: 6 grams, and Sugar: 3 grams.

VEGAN FALAFEL WRAP

A wrap filled with crispy falafel, fresh vegetables, and hummus.

- Prep Time: 20 minutes
- Cook Time: 20-25 minutes
- Total Time: 40-45 minutes
- Servings: 4

Ingredients:

For the Falafel:

- 15 oz chickpeas, drained and rinsed
- 1/2 onion, roughly chopped
- 2 cloves garlic, roughly chopped
- 1/2 cup fresh parsley leaves
- 1/2 cup fresh cilantro leaves
- 1 tsp cumin
- 1 tsp coriander
- 1 tsp salt
- 1/2 tsp black pepper
- 1/4 cup all-purpose flour or chickpea flour
- Oil for frying

For the Wrap:

- 4 large flour tortillas or wraps
- 1 cup of hummus
- 1/4 red onion, thinly sliced
- 1 large tomato, sliced
- 1 cucumber, sliced
- 1 cup of mixed greens
- Hot sauce (optional)

Directions:

1. Blend chickpeas, onion, garlic, parsley, cilantro, cumin, coriander, salt, and black pepper in a food processor until mixture is evenly combined with a slightly chunky texture.

41

2. After transferring the mixture into a mixing bowl, add all-purpose or chickpea flour to it. Mix the ingredients well until the mixture is firm and can hold its shape.

3. Shape the falafel mixture into balls, then slightly flatten them.

4. Using medium-high heat, warm the skillet with oil. When the oil is heated, place the falafel patties in the pan and cook for 4-5 minutes per side, until they turn crispy and golden brown. Alternatively, bake in the oven for 20-25 minutes.

5. Take out the falafel patties from the skillet and put them on paper towels to eliminate any excess oil.

6. To assemble the wrap, spread 1/4 cup of hummus onto each tortilla or wrap. Add 3-4 falafel patties to each wrap, along with sliced red onions, tomatoes, cucumbers, and mixed greens. Add hot sauce if desired.

7. Roll up the wrap tightly and serve.

Nutritional breakdown per serving (based on 4 servings):

Calories: 495 kcal, Protein: 0 grams, Carbohydrates: 0 grams, Fat: 1 grams, Saturated Fat: 2 grams, Cholesterol: 0 milligrams, Sodium: 1260 milligrams, Fiber: 0 grams, and Sugar: 1 grams.

VEGAN CHICKPEA TOMATO SOUP

A flavorful soup made with chickpeas and tomatoes.

- Prep Time: 10 minutes
- Cook Time: 30 minutes
- Total Time: 40 minutes
- Servings: 4

Ingredients:

- 1 tablespoon olive oil
- 1 large onion, diced
- 3 cloves garlic, minced
- 1/2 teaspoon dried thyme
- 1/2 teaspoon dried oregano
- 1/4 teaspoon red pepper flakes (optional)
- 1 can (14.5 ounces) diced tomatoes
- 4 cups vegetable broth
- 15 oz can chickpeas, drained and rinsed
- 1 cup uncooked quinoa
- Salt and black pepper to taste
- Fresh parsley leaves, chopped (optional)

Directions:

1. To start cooking, set a large pot or Dutch oven on medium heat and add a small amount of olive oil. Put in the diced onion and cook for approximately 5 minutes, until it turns translucent and tender.
2. Add the minced garlic, dried thyme, dried oregano, and red pepper flakes (if using). Continue cooking for 2 more minutes until a pleasant aroma develops.
3. Add the diced tomatoes and vegetable broth to the pot. Heat until it reaches a simmer and allow it to cook for 10 minutes.
4. Add the chickpeas and quinoa to the pot. Let it simmer for about 20-25 minutes, until the quinoa is cooked and soft.
5. Season with salt and black pepper as per your liking.
6. Serve hot, optionally garnished with chopped fresh parsley.

Nutritional breakdown per serving (based on 4 servings):

Calories: 340 kcal, Protein: 16 grams, Carbohydrates: 56 grams, Fat: 6 grams, Saturated Fat: 1 grams, Cholesterol: 0 milligrams, Sodium: 911 milligrams, Fiber: 11 grams, and Sugar: 7 grams.

VEGAN BLT SANDWICH

A classic sandwich made with tempeh bacon, lettuce, tomato, and vegan mayo.

- Prep Time: 10 minutes
- Cook Time: 15 minutes
- Total Time: 25 minutes
- Servings: 2

Ingredients:

- 6-8 slices of tofu bacon
- 4 slices of bread (vegan)
- 2-3 leaves of lettuce
- 1 medium-sized tomato, sliced
- 1 avocado, sliced
- 2 tablespoons vegan mayonnaise
- Salt and black pepper to taste

Directions:

1. Cook the tofu bacon according to package instructions until crispy and browned.
2. Toast the bread slices to your liking.
3. Spread vegan mayonnaise on each bread slice.
4. Layer the lettuce leaves on the bottom slice of bread, followed by tomato slices and avocado slices. Adjust the amount of salt and black pepper to your taste preference.
5. Add the cooked tofu bacon slices on top of the avocado and tomato slices.
6. Top with the other slice of bread and serve.

Nutritional breakdown per serving (based on 2 servings):

Calories: 470 kcal, Protein: 17 grams, Carbohydrates: 45 grams, Fat: 27 grams, Saturated Fat: 4 grams, Cholesterol: 0 milligrams, Sodium: 840 milligrams, Fiber: 13 grams, and Sugar: 6 grams.

VEGAN QUINOA STIR-FRY

A stir-fry with colorful vegetables and protein-packed quinoa.

- Prep Time: 10 minutes
- Cook Time: 20 minutes
- Total Time: 30 minutes
- Servings: 4

Ingredients:

- 1 cup quinoa
- 2 cups vegetable broth
- 1 tablespoon olive oil
- 1 medium onion, chopped
- 2 cloves garlic, minced
- 1 red bell pepper, sliced
- 1 yellow bell pepper, sliced
- 1 medium zucchini, sliced
- 1 cup frozen edamame
- 2 tablespoons soy sauce
- 2 tablespoons hoisin sauce
- 2 tablespoons cornstarch
- Salt and black pepper to taste

Directions:

1. Rinse the quinoa with cold water through a fine mesh strainer to remove any residue.
2. In a medium-sized saucepan, combine the quinoa and vegetable broth, then heat the mixture over medium heat until it starts to boil. After the mixture starts boiling, turn the heat down to low, cover the saucepan, and let it simmer for about 15 to 20 minutes, until all the liquid has been fully absorbed.
3. Take a large skillet, heat up the olive oil on medium heat, and then put in the chopped onion and garlic. Sauté the mixture for about 5 minutes, or until they are softened.
4. Include the sliced red and yellow bell peppers to the skillet and cook them further for approximately 5 minutes until they become tender.
5. Add the sliced zucchini and frozen edamame and cook for an additional 5 minutes.
6. Take a small bowl and blend together soy sauce, hoisin sauce, and cornstarch until they are thoroughly combined.

7. Drizzle the sauce over the vegetables and mix well, ensuring that everything is evenly coated.
8. If desired, sprinkle some fresh herbs as a garnish and serve it hot.

Nutritional breakdown per serving (based on 4 servings):

Calories: 268 kcal, Protein: 12 grams, Carbohydrates: 44 grams, Fat: 6 grams, Saturated Fat: 1 grams, Cholesterol: 0 milligrams, Sodium: 729 milligrams, Fiber: 8 grams, and Sugar: 8 grams.

VEGAN MUSHROOM AND SPINACH OMELETTE

A fluffy omelette filled with sautéed mushrooms and spinach.

- Prep Time: 10 minutes
- Cook Time: 15 minutes
- Total Time: 25 minutes
- Servings: 2

Ingredients:

- 1 tablespoon olive oil
- 1/2 cup sliced mushrooms
- 1 cup fresh spinach
- Salt and black pepper to taste
- 4 tablespoons nutritional yeast
- 1/2 cup unsweetened almond milk
- 1 tablespoon cornstarch
- 1/4 teaspoon garlic powder
- Fresh chives for garnish (optional)

Directions:

1. To initiate the process, place a non-stick skillet on medium heat and pour some olive oil on it. Once heated, add the sliced mushrooms to the skillet and sauté them for approximately 5 minutes until they're nicely browned and softened.
2. Add fresh spinach to the skillet and sauté for an additional 2-3 minutes until wilted.
3. After preparing the mushroom and spinach mixture, you should season it with salt and pepper according to your taste. Afterwards, move the mixture to a plate.
4. Combine nutritional yeast, almond milk, cornstarch, garlic powder, salt, and pepper in a small bowl and whisk until the mixture is smooth and well-blended.
5. Once again heat the skillet to medium and add the almond milk mixture. Keep stirring constantly and cook for around 2 to 3 minutes until the mixture thickens.
6. Pour the mushroom and spinach mixture over one half of the omelette, and use a spatula to fold the other half of the omelette over the filling.
7. Cook for an additional 1-2 minutes until the omelette is fully cooked.
8. Serve hot, optionally garnished with fresh chives.

Nutritional breakdown per serving (based on 2 servings):

Calories: 156 kcal, Protein: 12 grams, Carbohydrates: 8 grams, Fat: 10 grams, Saturated Fat: 1 grams, Cholesterol: 0 milligrams, Sodium: 172 milligrams, Fiber: 3 grams, and Sugar: 1 grams.

VEGAN SWEET POTATO AND BLACK BEAN QUESADILLA

A tasty quesadilla filled with sweet potatoes and black beans.

- Prep Time: 15 minutes
- Cook Time: 15 minutes
- Total Time: 30 minutes
- Servings: 4

Ingredients:

- Dice 2 sweet potatoes into small cubes after peeling.
- 1 can black beans, drained and rinsed
- 1/2 teaspoon chili powder
- 1/2 teaspoon cumin
- Salt and pepper to taste
- 4 tortillas (use vegan if desired)
- 1 cup vegan shredded cheese
- Salsa, guacamole, or vegan sour cream for serving (optional)

Directions:

1. Preheat the oven to 400°F.
2. Put chopped sweet potatoes and a splash of water into a large skillet on medium heat. Cover the skillet with a lid and let cook for about 5-7 minutes or until the sweet potatoes are tender.
3. Combine the black beans, chili powder, cumin, salt, and pepper in the skillet and stir. Cook for an additional 2-3 minutes or until the beans are heated through.
4. Lay out the tortillas and sprinkle each with vegan shredded cheese.
5. Spoon the sweet potato and black bean mixture on one half of the tortilla, leaving some space around the edges.
6. Fold the other half of the tortilla over the filling.
7. Arrange the filled tortillas on a baking sheet and place it in the oven to bake for 8-10 minutes, or until the cheese has melted and the tortillas' texture has turned crispy.
8. Serve hot, optionally served with salsa, guacamole, or vegan sour cream.

Nutritional breakdown per serving (based on 4 servings):

Calories: 385 kcal, Protein: 16 grams, Carbohydrates: 60 grams, Fat: 11 grams, Saturated Fat: 4 grams, Cholesterol: 0 milligrams, Sodium: 662 milligrams, Fiber: 13 grams, and Sugar: 8 grams.

VEGAN ROASTED RED PEPPER PASTA

A creamy pasta dish made with roasted red peppers and plant-based cream.

- Prep Time: 15 minutes
- Cook Time: 30 minutes
- Total Time: 45 minutes
- Servings: 4

Ingredients:

- 2 red bell peppers, roasted and stripped of skin, each one big in size
- 1 pound pasta (use vegan if desired)
- 1 tablespoon olive oil
- 1 onion, chopped
- 3 cloves garlic, minced
- 1/2 teaspoon red pepper flakes
- Salt and black pepper to taste
- 1/2 cup vegetable broth
- 1/4 cup nutritional yeast
- Fresh parsley for garnish (optional)

Directions:

1. Preheat the oven to 425°F. Cut the red peppers in half and remove the stems, seeds, and white membranes. Lay the pepper halves with the flat side facing down on a baking sheet, then put the sheet inside the oven and roast them for around 20 to 25 minutes.
2. Take out the roasted peppers from the oven and move them to a plastic bag. Seal the bag and let the peppers sit for 10-15 minutes to steam. After this time has passed, remove the peppers from the bag and peel off the skin. Chop the peppers into coarse pieces and keep them aside.
3. Prepare the pasta based on the directions on the package, then keep it aside.
4. As the pasta is cooking, place a large skillet over medium heat and heat the olive oil in it. Add the chopped onion and sauté for 3-5 minutes until translucent.
5. Include the minced garlic, red pepper flakes, salt, and black pepper in the skillet, and cook for another 1-2 minutes until fragrance develops.
6. Add the vegetable broth and nutritional yeast to the blender with the mixture, and blend until it achieves a smooth consistency.

7. Move the mixture to a blender together with the vegetable broth and nutritional yeast. Blend until the texture becomes smooth.
8. Return the sauce to the skillet and heat over low heat.
9. Mix the sauce and the cooked pasta together in the skillet, and softly toss until the pasta is coated evenly.
10. Serve hot, optionally garnished with fresh parsley.

Nutritional breakdown per serving (based on 4 servings):

Calories: 350 kcal, Protein: 11 grams, Carbohydrates: 68 grams, Fat: 5 grams, Saturated Fat: 1 grams, Cholesterol: 0 milligrams, Sodium: 200 milligrams, Fiber: 5 grams, and Sugar: 11 grams.

VEGAN AVOCADO TOAST

Toast topped with smashed avocado and a variety of toppings.

- Prep Time: 10 minutes
- Cook Time: 0 minutes
- Total Time: 10 minutes
- Servings: 2

Ingredients:

- 2 slices of whole-grain bread (use vegan if desired)
- 1 ripe avocado
- 1 small tomato, diced
- 1/2 teaspoon garlic powder
- Salt and pepper to taste
- Optional toppings: red pepper flakes, vegan cheese, sliced radish, nutritional yeast

Directions:

1. Toast the slices of bread until crispy.
2. As the bread is toasting, slice the avocado in half lengthwise, take out the pit, and transfer the flesh into a small bowl. Gently press the avocado with a fork until it achieves a smooth consistency.
3. Combine the diced tomato, garlic powder, salt, and pepper with the mashed avocado in the bowl, and stir until thoroughly mixed.
4. Incorporate any other toppings you prefer, such as vegan cheese, red pepper flakes, nutritional yeast, or sliced radish.
5. Incorporate any other toppings you prefer, such as vegan cheese, red pepper flakes, nutritional yeast, or sliced radish.
6. Serve immediately.

Nutritional breakdown per serving (based on 2 servings):

Calories: 211 kcal, Protein: 5 grams, Carbohydrates: 24 grams, Fat: 12 grams, Saturated Fat: 2 grams, Cholesterol: 0 milligrams, Sodium: 120 milligrams, Fiber: 7 grams, and Sugar: 5 grams.

LENTIL AND ROASTED VEGETABLE SALAD

Lentil and roasted vegetable salad is a wholesome and flavorful dish featuring protein-packed lentils and a variety of roasted vegetables. This salad is both nutritious and fulfilling, making it an ideal option as either a main course or a side dish.

- Preparation Time: 15 minutes
- Cooking Time: 30-40 minutes
- Total Time: Approximately 50-55 minutes
- Servings: 4

Ingredients:

- 1 cup of brown or green lentils
- 1 red onion, chopped
- 1 bell pepper, seeded and chopped
- 2 cups of seasonal root vegetables, chopped (such as carrots, parsnips, or sweet potatoes)
- 4 cloves of garlic, minced
- 2 tablespoons of olive oil
- 1 teaspoon of paprika
- Salt and pepper, to taste
- 2 cups of mixed greens
- 1/2 cup of crumbled feta cheese
- A handful of freshly chopped parsley

Directions:

1. Preheat the oven to 400°F.
2. Rinse the lentils under cold water and drain. In a saucepan, boil the lentils in 2 cups of water until tender, about 20-30 minutes. Drain and set aside.
3. Mix together the onion, bell pepper, root vegetables, garlic, olive oil, paprika, salt, and pepper in a mixing bowl until they are evenly coated with the seasonings.
4. Evenly distribute the vegetables on a lined baking sheet, making sure to keep them in a single layer. Roast the vegetables in the oven for roughly 20-30 minutes, or until they are tender and have developed a slight browning on the surface.
5. Combine the cooked lentils and roasted vegetables in a mixing bowl. Toss with mixed greens.
6. Before serving, add some crumbled feta cheese and freshly chopped parsley on top of the salad. Bon appétit!

Nutritional breakdown per serving:

Calories: 360 kcal, Protein: 18 grams, Carbohydrates: 47 grams, Fat: 12 grams, Saturated Fat: 5 grams, Sodium: 17 milligrams, Fiber: 15 grams, and Sugar: 7 grams.

VEGGIE WRAP

A wrap stuffed with hummus, vegetables, and your preferred protein option (for example tofu or tempeh).

- Prep Time: 10 minutes
- Cook Time: 0 minutes
- Total Time: 10 minutes
- Servings: 2

Ingredients:

- 2 large whole wheat or gluten-free tortillas
- 1/2 cup hummus
- 1/2 red bell pepper, thinly sliced
- 1/2 yellow squash, thinly sliced
- 1/2 zucchini, thinly sliced
- 1/2 cup alfalfa sprouts
- 1/2 avocado, sliced
- Salt and pepper to taste

Directions:

1. Lay the tortillas on a flat surface.
2. Spread the hummus evenly over the tortillas.
3. Layer the sliced red bell pepper, yellow squash, and zucchini on top of the hummus.
4. Add the alfalfa sprouts and sliced avocado.
5. Sprinkle with salt and pepper to taste.
6. Roll up the tortillas tightly, tucking in the sides as you go.
7. Cut each wrap in half diagonally.
8. After serving, if desired, tightly wrap in plastic wrap and place in the refrigerator for later consumption.

Nutritional breakdown per serving (based on 2 servings):

Calories: 414 kcal, Protein: 15 grams, Carbohydrates: 42 grams, Fat: 22 grams, Saturated Fat: 3 grams, Cholesterol: 0 milligrams, Sodium: 581 milligrams, Fiber: 15 grams, and Sugar: 4 grams.

STUFFED BELL PEPPERS

Bell peppers stuffed with rice, beans, and veggies, topped with a sprinkle of plant-based cheese.

- Prep Time: 30 minutes
- Cook Time: 1 hour 30 minutes
- Total Time: 2 hours
- Servings: 6

Ingredients:

- 6 large bell peppers, tops removed and seeds removed
- 1 pound ground beef or ground turkey
- 1 cup cooked brown rice
- 1 small onion, diced
- 2 cloves garlic, minced
- 1 can (14 oz) diced tomatoes, drained
- 1 can (8 oz) tomato sauce
- 1 tablespoon Worcestershire sauce
- Salt and black pepper to taste
- 1/4 cup chopped fresh parsley
- 1/4 cup grated Parmesan cheese

Directions:

1. Preheat the oven to 350°F.
2. In a large skillet, cook the ground beef or turkey over medium heat until browned.
3. Put the onion and garlic in the skillet and sauté until they become soft.
4. Combine the brown rice, diced tomatoes, tomato sauce, Worcestershire sauce, salt, and pepper in the skillet containing the cooked ingredients. Stir until everything is well combined and heated through.
5. Stuff each bell pepper with the mixture from the skillet and place in a baking dish.
6. Top the peppers with any remaining filling mixture.
7. Put the filled peppers in the oven that has already been heated and bake them for 1 to 1 and a half hours, or until the peppers are tender and the filling is thoroughly heated.
8. Sprinkle each pepper with chopped parsley and grated Parmesan cheese before serving.

Nutritional breakdown per serving (based on 6 servings):

Calories: 293 kcal, Protein: 22 grams, Carbohydrates: 52 grams, Fat: 11 grams, Saturated Fat: 4 grams, Cholesterol: 52 milligrams, Sodium: 411 milligrams, Fiber: 5 grams, and Sugar: 7 grams.

CHICKPEA SALAD

A simple salad made with chickpeas, cucumbers, tomatoes, and a lemon-tahini dressing.

- Prep Time: 15 minutes
- Cook Time: 0 minutes
- Total Time: 15 minutes
- Servings: 4

Ingredients:

- 2 cans (30 oz) chickpeas, drained
- 1 red bell pepper, diced
- 1/2 red onion, diced
- 1/2 cup chopped fresh parsley
- 1/4 cup chopped fresh mint
- 1/4 cup extra-virgin olive oil
- 1/4 cup freshly squeezed lemon juice
- 1 teaspoon ground cumin
- Salt and black pepper to taste

Directions:

1. Put together the chickpeas, red bell pepper, red onion, parsley, and mint into a large mixing bowl and blend thoroughly.
2. Combine the olive oil, lemon juice, cumin, salt, and pepper in a small bowl and whisk them together.
3. Drizzle the dressing over the chickpea mixture and mix everything well until it is evenly coated.
4. You can choose to either serve the food immediately or place it in the fridge for one to two hours to let the flavors combine before serving.

Nutritional breakdown per serving (based on 4 servings):

Calories: 367 kcal, Protein: 14 grams, Carbohydrates: 40 grams, Fat: 17 grams, Saturated Fat: 2 grams, Cholesterol: 0 milligrams, Sodium: 477 milligrams, Fiber: 11 grams, and Sugar: 7 grams.

PASTA SALAD

A flavorful pasta salad with a variety of veggies and a tangy vinaigrette dressing.

- Prep Time: 20 minutes
- Cook Time: 10 minutes
- Additional Time: 8 hours (for chilling)
- Total Time: 8 hours 30 minutes
- Servings: 6

Ingredients:

- 1 pound dry rotini pasta
- 1 cup cherry tomatoes, halved
- 1 cup cucumber, diced
- 1 cup bell pepper, diced
- 1/2 cup red onion, diced
- 1/2 cup black olives, sliced
- 1/2 cup feta cheese, crumbled
- 1/4 cup extra-virgin olive oil
- 1/4 cup red wine vinegar
- 1 teaspoon dried oregano
- Salt and black pepper to taste

Directions:

1. Prepare the pasta as per the instructions on the package, then drain it and rinse with cold water.
2. In a large mixing bowl, toss together the cooked pasta, cherry tomatoes, cucumber, bell pepper, red onion, black olives, and feta cheese.
3. Mix together the olive oil, red wine vinegar, dried oregano, salt, and pepper in a small bowl using a whisk.
4. Add the dressing to the pasta mixture, then mix until the dressing covers the mixture completely.
5. If you want to intensify the flavor, it's advisable to cover the bowl with plastic wrap and refrigerate it for at least 8 hours. For optimal results, you can leave it in the fridge overnight.
6. Serve chilled and enjoy!

Nutritional breakdown per serving (based on 6 servings):

Calories: 470 kcal, Protein: 14 grams, Carbohydrates: 17 grams, Fat: 4 grams, Saturated Fat: 4 grams, Cholesterol: 17 milligrams, Sodium: 323 milligrams, Fiber: 5 grams, and Sugar: 4 grams.

VEGAN TERIYAKI TOFU BOWL

A filling bowl with protein-packed tofu, vegetables, and a sweet and savory teriyaki sauce.

- Prep Time: 15 minutes
- Cook Time: 20 minutes
- Total Time: 35 minutes
- Servings: 4

Ingredients:

- 1 cup brown rice, uncooked
- 1 block (14 oz) extra-firm tofu, drained and pressed
- 1 tablespoon cornstarch
- 1 tablespoon vegetable oil
- 1/4 cup soy sauce
- 1/4 cup mirin
- 1 tablespoon rice vinegar
- 2 tablespoons brown sugar
- 1 teaspoon grated ginger
- 1 garlic clove, minced
- 4 cups mixed vegetables (snap peas, carrots, bell peppers, etc.)
- Garnish with sesame seeds and green onions

Directions:

1. In a medium pot, cook the brown rice according to the package instructions.
2. Dice the pressed tofu into evenly sized 1-inch cubes, and then coat them with a layer of cornstarch.
3. Using a non-stick skillet, heat up some vegetable oil over medium-high heat. Then, add the diced tofu and cook it for a total of 5 to 7 minutes, flipping it occasionally, until the tofu becomes crispy and turns a golden brown color.
4. Meanwhile, in a small bowl, whisk together the soy sauce, mirin, rice vinegar, brown sugar, ginger, and garlic.
5. Add the mixed vegetables to the skillet with the tofu and cook for an additional 3-5 minutes, until tender-crisp.
6. After the tofu and vegetables are fully cooked, pour a generous amount of teriyaki sauce over them and stir well. Let the mixture simmer for another 1-2 minutes until the sauce achieves the thickness you desire.

7. Once that's done, divide the cooked rice evenly between four bowls and add a portion of the tofu and vegetable mixture on top of each. Before serving, sprinkle some sesame seeds and sliced green onions over the top as a garnish.

Nutritional breakdown per serving (based on 4 servings):

Calories: 464 kcal, Protein: 17 grams, Carbohydrates: 75 grams, Fat: 13 grams, Saturated Fat: 1 grams, Cholesterol: 0 milligrams, Sodium: 1.046 milligrams, Fiber: 7 grams, and Sugar: 12 grams.

VEGAN BLACK BEAN SOUP

A hearty and flavorful soup made with black beans and spices.

- Prep Time: 15 minutes
- Cook Time: 30 minutes
- Total Time: 45 minutes
- Servings: 6

Ingredients:

- 2 tablespoons olive oil
- 1 onion, chopped
- 2 cloves garlic, minced
- 2 teaspoons ground cumin
- 1 teaspoon smoked paprika
- 1/4 teaspoon cayenne pepper
- 4 cups vegetable broth
- 2 (15 oz) cans black beans, drained and rinsed
- 1 can (14.5 oz) diced tomatoes, undrained
- Juice of 1 lime
- Salt and black pepper to taste
- Optional toppings: avocado, diced tomatoes, sliced green onions, cilantro, sour cream or vegan sour cream, tortilla chips

Directions:

1. Using a large pot, heat up some olive oil over medium heat.
2. Heat a sizable pot using medium heat and pour in some olive oil.
3. Include the cumin, smoked paprika, and cayenne pepper, then sauté for another minute, until they release an enticing aroma.
4. Add the vegetable broth, black beans, and diced tomatoes with their juices to the mixture, then stir them together until everything is fully combined.
5. Gently heat up the soup and let it cook on a simmer for 20 to 25 minutes. This will help the different flavors come together and the soup to thicken slightly.
6. Add the lime juice to the mixture and season it with appropriate amount of salt and black pepper according to your personal taste. Ensure that all ingredients are well combined.
7. Serve hot, with your favorite toppings.

Nutritional breakdown per serving (based on 6 servings):

Calories: 139 kcal, Protein: 7 grams, Carbohydrates: 21 grams, Fat: 4 grams, Saturated Fat: 1 grams, Cholesterol: 0 milligrams, Sodium: 787 milligrams, Fiber: 8 grams, and Sugar: 3 grams.

VEGAN STUFFED BELL PEPPERS

Vegan Stuffed Bell Peppers are flavorful and colorful bell peppers filled with protein-packed ingredients such as quinoa , rice, and lentils, and topped with vegan cheese or breadcrumbs. This dish can be customized and enjoyed as a nutritious main meal or a side dish.

- Preparation Time: 20 minutes
- Cooking Time: 1 hour
- Total Time: 1 hour and 20 minutes
- Servings: 4

Ingredients:

- 4 large bell peppers, halved lengthwise and seeds removed
- 1 cup of brown rice
- 1 can black beans, drained and rinsed
- 1 medium onion, chopped
- 2 garlic cloves, minced
- 1 tablespoon of olive oil
- 1/4 cup of chopped fresh parsley
- 1/4 cup of chopped fresh cilantro
- 1/4 teaspoon of cumin
- Salt and pepper, to taste
- 1 cup of tomato sauce

Directions:

1. Preheat the oven to 375°F.
2. In a saucepan, cook the brown rice according to package instructions. Set aside.
3. Place a skillet over the burner on medium heat, then drizzle some olive oil over its surface. After it's heated up, sauté the onion and garlic in the skillet for around 3-4 minutes or until they turn tender.
4. Add the black beans, parsley, cilantro, cumin, salt, and pepper. Cook for an additional 3-5 minutes.
5. Combine the cooked rice and black bean mixture in a mixing bowl.
6. Stuff the halved bell peppers with the rice and black bean mixture.
7. Arrange the stuffed bell peppers inside a baking dish and pour the tomato sauce generously over them.

8. Securely cover the dish with aluminum foil, then place it in the oven and bake at a temperature of 350°F for approximately 45-60 minutes or until the stuffed peppers have become soft in texture and the filling has been fully heated.
9. Remove from the oven and let cool for a few minutes before serving. Enjoy!

Nutritional breakdown per serving:

Calories: 329 kcal, Protein: 7 grams, Carbohydrates: 55 grams, Fat: 11 grams, Saturated Fat: 1 grams, Sodium: 57 milligrams, Fiber: 14 grams, and Sugar: 25 grams.

VEGAN CAESAR SALAD WRAP

Enjoy a wrap containing crisp lettuce and a rich vegan Caesar sauce.

- Prep Time: 20 minutes
- Cook Time: 0 minutes
- Total Time: 20 minutes
- Servings: 2

Ingredients:

- 1 head romaine lettuce, chopped
- 1/2 cup croutons (make sure they are vegan)
- 1/4 cup vegan parmesan cheese
- Caesar dressing (you can make your own or use a store-bought vegan version)
- 2 large wraps (choose your favorite type, such as whole wheat, spinach, or tomato)

Directions:

1. In a large bowl, mix together the chopped romaine lettuce, croutons, and vegan parmesan cheese.
2. Drizzle Caesar dressing over the salad mixture, and toss to coat.
3. Lay a wrap on a clean surface, and place half of the salad mixture in the center of the wrap.
4. Tuck in the sides of the wrap, and roll up tightly.
5. Repeat with the remaining wrap and salad mixture.
6. Cut the wraps in half and serve without delay.

Nutritional breakdown per serving (based on 2 servings):

Calories: 304 kcal, Protein: 8 grams, Carbohydrates: 30 grams, Fat: 17 grams, Saturated Fat: 3 grams, Cholesterol: 0 milligrams, Sodium: 565 milligrams, Fiber: 6 grams, and Sugar: 8 grams.

VEGAN LENTIL AND RICE BOWL

A bowl filled with protein-packed lentils, rice, and fresh vegetables.

- Prep Time: 15 minutes
- Cook Time: 35 minutes
- Total Time: 50 minutes
- Servings: 4

Ingredients:

- 1 cup brown or black lentils, uncooked
- 1 cup brown rice, uncooked
- 2 cloves garlic, minced
- 1 onion, chopped
- 1 carrot, sliced
- 1 red bell pepper, chopped
- 1 tablespoon olive oil
- 2 teaspoons ground cumin
- 1/2 teaspoon smoked paprika
- Salt and pepper to taste
- 4 cups vegetable broth or water
- Optional toppings: avocado, cilantro, diced tomatoes, hot sauce

Directions:

1. Use a large pot and warm up the olive oil on medium heat.
2. Introduce the diced onion and finely chopped garlic into the pot, sautéing for approximately 2 to 3 minutes, or until the onion achieves a soft and translucent texture.
3. Introduce the cut carrots and chopped red bell peppers to the pot and continue cooking for another 2 to 3 minutes.
4. Add the uncooked rice, uncooked lentils, cumin, smoked paprika, salt, and pepper to the pot. Mix well to ensure the vegetables and grains are evenly coated.
5. Add either vegetable broth or water to the mixture and increase the heat to high, allowing it to boil. After boiling the mixture, bring down the heat to low and tightly cover the pot with a fitting lid.
6. Simmer the lentil and rice mixture for 30 minutes, or until the grains are tender and the liquid has been absorbed.

7. Take the pot off the heat and let the mixture rest for another 5 minutes while keeping it covered.
8. Fluff the lentil and rice mixture with a fork, and serve hot in bowls.
9. Incorporate your preferred toppings like diced avocado, cilantro, or hot sauce to enhance the flavor.

Nutritional breakdown per serving (based on 4 servings):

Calories: 390 kcal, Protein: 18 grams, Carbohydrates: 69 grams, Fat: 7 grams, Saturated Fat: 1 grams, Cholesterol: 0 milligrams, Sodium: 676 milligrams, Fiber: 15 grams, and Sugar: 5 grams.

SWEET POTATO BUDDHA BOWL

A hearty bowl filled with roasted sweet potatoes, quinoa, avocado, and veggies.

- Prep Time: 15 minutes
- Cook Time: 30 minutes
- Total Time: 45 minutes
- Servings: 4

Ingredients:

- 2 choped medium sweet potatoes into small pieces after peeling them
- 1 can of chickpeas, drained and rinsed
- 1/2 teaspoon chili powder
- 1/4 teaspoon paprika
- Salt and pepper to taste
- 4 cups kale, chopped and stems removed
- 1 red onion, sliced thinly
- 2 tablespoons olive oil
- 1/4 cup tahini
- 2 tablespoons lemon juice
- 2 tablespoons maple syrup
- 2 cloves garlic, minced
- 1/4 teaspoon salt
- Black pepper to taste
- 1/4 cup pumpkin seeds
- 1 avocado, sliced thinly

Directions:

1. Adjust the oven to preheat at 400°F (205°C) and make sure to set the temperature appropriately.
2. Arrange the cut sweet potatoes onto a baking sheet covered with parchment paper. Apply 1 tablespoon of olive oil over the top, then season with salt and black pepper. Roast in the oven for about 25-30 minutes, flipping the pieces over halfway through.
3. During the sweet potatoes' cooking process, you may begin the preparation of the chickpeas.Simply grab a small bowl and mix the chickpeas with chili powder, paprika, salt, and black pepper by gently tossing them.

4. Place the chickpeas on a separate baking sheet lined with parchment paper. Bake in the oven for 20 minutes, or until crispy, shaking the tray occasionally to prevent sticking.
5. In a large bowl, mix together the chopped kale and sliced onions. Proceed by applying the rest of the olive oil and massaging the kale until it becomes soft.
6. In a small bowl, whisk together the tahini, lemon juice, maple syrup, minced garlic, salt, and black pepper to create the dressing.
7. Once the sweet potatoes and chickpeas are done, assemble the Buddha bowls. Divide the kale and onion mixture evenly between four bowls.
8. Place the roasted sweet potatoes and chickpeas on the top of each bowl.
9. Drizzle the bowls with tahini dressing.
10. Garnish each bowl with pumpkin seeds and sliced avocado.

Nutritional breakdown per serving (based on 4 servings):

Calories: 438 kcal, Protein: 0 grams, Carbohydrates: 0 grams, Fat: 24 grams, Saturated Fat: 3.3 grams, Cholesterol: 0 milligrams, Sodium: 335 milligrams, Fiber: 0 grams, and Sugar: 0 grams.

VEGAN MEDITERRANEAN VEGGIE WRAP WITH HUMMUS

Preparation Time: 10 minutes

Cooking Time: 0 minutes

Total Time: 10 minutes

Servings: 4

Ingredients:

- 4 large whole wheat or spinach tortillas
- 1 cup of hummus
- 2 cups of mixed salad greens
- 1/2 cup of sliced cucumber
- 1/2 cup sliced roasted red peppers
- 1/2 cup of sliced Kalamata olives
- 1/4 cup of crumbled feta cheese
- Salt and pepper, to taste

Directions:

1. Lay out tortillas and spread 1/4 cup of hummus on each tortilla.
2. Place mixed salad greens on top of the hummus layer.
3. Add sliced cucumber, roasted red peppers, and Kalamata olives to the wrap.
4. Sprinkle crumbled feta cheese over the veggies.
5. Add salt and pepper to taste.
6. Roll the wrap firmly, then slice it into two halves. Serve right away and savor the delicious taste!

Nutritional breakdown per serving:

Calories: 354 kcal, Protein: 14 grams, Carbohydrates: 42 grams, Fat: 16 grams, Saturated Fat: 9 grams, Sodium: 11 milligrams, Fiber: 10 grams, and Sugar: 4 grams.

BROCCOLI AND QUINOA BOWL

A nutritious bowl filled with roasted broccoli, quinoa, and a variety of veggies, all topped with a drizzle of tahini sauce.

- Prep Time: 15 minutes
- Cook Time: 25 minutes
- Total Time: 40 minutes
- Servings: 4

Ingredients:

- 1 cup quinoa, rinsed well
- 2 cups water or vegetable broth
- 4 cups broccoli florets
- 1 red onion, sliced
- 2 tablespoons olive oil
- Salt and pepper to taste
- 1 avocado, sliced
- 1/4 cup pumpkin seeds
- Lemon wedges, for serving

For the dressing:

- 1/4 cup tahini
- 2 tablespoons lemon juice
- 1 tablespoon honey or maple syrup
- 1 clove garlic, minced
- 1/4 teaspoon salt
- 1/4 cup warm water

Directions:

1. Combine the quinoa with either water or vegetable broth in a saucepan and bring to a boiling point.
2. Simmer the covered quinoa on low heat for 15 minutes until it's tender and all the liquid is absorbed.
3. As the quinoa cooks, start preheating your oven to 400°F (205°C).

4. In a big bowl, toss broccoli florets and sliced red onion using 2 tablespoons of olive oil. Customize the seasoning with salt and black pepper according to your liking. Mix thoroughly until the vegetables are coated evenly.
5. Heat the oven to the required temperature and cover a baking sheet with parchment paper. Spread the mix of broccoli and onion over the sheet evenly. Roast for 20-25 minutes, until the vegetables turn tender and get a light brown color.
6. Once the quinoa and roasted vegetables are done, assemble the bowls. Divide the quinoa between four bowls.
7. Top each bowl with the roasted broccoli and onion mixture.
8. Garnish each bowl with avocado slices and pumpkin seeds.
9. For making the dressing, simply whisk together tahini, lemon juice, minced garlic, honey or maple syrup, and salt until smooth. Add the warm water as needed to thin the dressing to your desired consistency.
10. Drizzle the dressing over the bowls.
11. Serve with lemon wedges, if desired.

Nutritional breakdown per serving (based on 4 servings):

Calories: 441 kcal, Protein: 0 grams, Carbohydrates: 44 grams, Fat: 26 grams, Saturated Fat: 3 grams, Cholesterol: 0 milligrams, Sodium: 198 milligrams, Fiber: 11 grams, and Sugar: 8 grams.

VEGGIE BURRITO BOWL

A filling and satisfying bowl with rice, beans, veggies, and your choice of protein (such as grilled veggies or tofu).

- Prep time: 20 minutes
- Cook time: 20 minutes
- Total time: 40 minutes
- Servings: 4

Ingredients:

- 1 cup brown rice
- 1 can black beans, drained and rinsed
- 1 red bell pepper, sliced
- 1 small red onion, sliced
- 2 cups corn, fresh or frozen
- 1 avocado, diced
- 1/4 cup cilantro, chopped
- Juice of 1 lime
- Salt to taste

For the seasoning:

- 1 tablespoon olive oil
- 1 tablespoon chili powder
- 1 teaspoon ground cumin
- 1/2 teaspoon garlic powder
- 1/2 teaspoon onion powder
- 1/4 teaspoon cayenne pepper
- 1/4 teaspoon salt
- 1/4 teaspoon black pepper

Directions:

1. Prepare the brown rice as per the instructions given on the package.
2. As the rice is being cooked, take a large skillet and start heating olive oil over a medium flame.
3. Cook the sliced red onion and bell pepper by sautéing them over medium heat for 5 to 7 minutes until they attain a tender, lightly browned appearance.

4. Add the black beans and corn to the skillet.
5. Put the chili powder, cumin, cayenne pepper, garlic powder, onion powder, black pepper, and salt in the skillet with the vegetables. Stir well to evenly coat the seasoning over the vegetables.
6. Sauté for an additional 5-7 minutes, or until the vegetables are cooked through and the flavors have melded together.
7. In a petite bowl, mix the diced avocado, cilantro, and lime juice. Stir well until everything is evenly combined.
8. Once the rice and vegetables are done, assemble the bowls. Divide the rice between four bowls.
9. Top each bowl with the vegetable mixture.
10. Garnish each bowl with the avocado mixture.
11. Serve warm.

Nutritional breakdown per serving (based on 4 servings):

Calories: 365 kcal, Protein: 0 grams, Carbohydrates: 61 grams, Fat: 11 grams, Saturated Fat: 1 grams, Cholesterol: 0 milligrams, Sodium: 407 milligrams, Fiber: 17 grams, and Sugar: 8 grams.

CHICKPEA AND VEGETABLE CURRY

Chickpea and Vegetable Curry is a healthy and flavorful vegetarian dish that can be customized using a variety of vegetables and spices. Usually prepared with chickpeas, this curry is abundant in protein and is best enjoyed with rice or naan bread, making for a nourishing and gratifying meal.

- Preparation Time: 15 minutes
- Cooking Time: 40 minutes
- Total Time: 55 minutes
- Servings: 4

Ingredients:

- 1 tablespoon of olive oil
- 1 large onion, chopped
- 4 cloves of garlic, minced
- 1 tablespoon of fresh grated ginger
- 2 large carrots, chopped
- 1 red bell pepper, chopped
- 1 small zucchini, chopped
- 1 can of chickpeas, drained and rinsed
- 1 can of diced tomatoes
- 1 tablespoon of curry powder
- 1 teaspoon of ground cumin
- 1/2 teaspoon of ground cinnamon
- 1/4 teaspoon of cayenne pepper
- 1 cup of vegetable broth
- Salt and pepper, to taste
- Fresh cilantro, for serving (optional)

Directions:

1. To initiate the cooking process, heat up some olive oil in a Dutch oven or large pot on the stove at medium-high temperature.
2. Put chopped onion, garlic, and ginger in the pan and sauté them for approximately 5-7 minutes until the onions become translucent and soft.
3. Introduce the chopped carrots, red bell pepper, and zucchini. Cook them until they are lightly softened for about 5 minutes.

4. Add the chickpeas, diced tomatoes, curry powder, ground cumin, ground cinnamon, and cayenne pepper. Stir well to combine.
5. Pour the vegetable broth into the mixture and bring it to a boil. Next, reduce the heat and let it gently simmer for about 25-30 minutes until the sauce thickens, and the vegetables become soft to the touch.
6. Season with salt and pepper to taste.
7. Serve hot, garnished with fresh cilantro if desired.

Nutritional breakdown per serving:

Calories: 234 kcal, Protein: 10 grams, Carbohydrates: 39 grams, Fat: 12 grams, Saturated Fat: 6 grams, Sodium: 15 milligrams, Fiber: 12 grams, and Sugar: 14 grams.

VEGAN SWEET POTATO CURRY

A flavorful curry made with sweet potatoes, spices, and coconut milk.

- Prep time: 15 minutes
- Cook time: 30 minutes
- Total time: 45 minutes
- Servings: 4

Ingredients:

- 2 large sweet potatoes, peeled and chopped
- 1 red onion, diced
- 1 red bell pepper, diced
- 3 cloves garlic, minced
- 1 tablespoon grated fresh ginger
- 2 tablespoons red curry paste
- 1 (13.5 oz) can coconut milk
- 1/4 cup vegetable broth
- 2 cups baby spinach leaves
- Salt and pepper to taste
- Fresh cilantro, chopped (for serving)

Directions:

1. Take a large pan or Dutch oven and heat up some oil over medium heat.
2. Add the diced onion and bell pepper, garlic, and grated ginger. Cook until the vegetables become tender, which should take approximately 5 minutes.
3. Next, include the sweet potatoes and keep the vegetables cooking for an additional 5 minutes.
4. Introduce the red curry paste, blend it thoroughly until it's coated on all the vegetables.
5. Include both the vegetable broth and coconut milk to your pot, and mix well until they're thoroughly combined.
6. Reduce the heat to low and let the curry simmer for about 20 minutes. Keep stirring occasionally until the sweet potatoes are fork-tender.
7. Put in the baby spinach and stir until it wilts. After that, remove the curry from the heat.
8. Season the curry with salt and pepper. Top off with a sprig of fresh cilantro and serve hot with either rice or naan bread.

Nutritional breakdown per serving (based on 4 servings):

Calories: 323 kcal, Protein: 4 grams, Carbohydrates: 33 grams, Fat: 20 grams, Saturated Fat: 17 grams, Cholesterol: 0 milligrams, Sodium: 285 milligrams, Fiber: 6 grams, and Sugar: 8 grams.

VEGAN CHICKPEA SALAD SANDWICH

A satisfying sandwich filled with chickpea salad and fresh vegetables.

- Prep time: 10 minutes
- Cook time: 0 minutes
- Total time: 10 minutes
- Servings: 2-3

Ingredients:

- 15 oz can of chickpeas, drained
- 2 stalks celery, diced
- 2 green onions, sliced
- 2 tablespoons vegan mayo
- 1 tablespoon Dijon mustard
- 1 tablespoon lemon juice
- Salt and pepper, to taste
- 4-6 slices whole-grain bread
- Lettuce, tomato, and avocado slices (optional)

Directions:

1. Take a large mixing bowl and use a fork or a potato masher to partially mash the chickpeas to still remain in chunks.
2. Add the diced celery and sliced green onions to the bowl and stir to combine.
3. Combine vegan mayo, Dijon mustard, and lemon juice in a small mixing bowl.
4. Evenly coat all ingredients by pouring the dressing onto the chickpea mixture and thoroughly mixing them together.
5. Add salt and pepper to the chickpea salad according to your preference.
6. To assemble the sandwich, toast the bread (if desired) and spread some extra vegan mayo on each slice.
7. Pile the chickpea salad onto one slice of the bread, then add lettuce, tomato, and avocado slices (if desired).
8. Top the sandwich with another slice of bread, cut in half, and serve.

Nutritional breakdown per serving (based on 3 servings):

Calories: 229 kcal, Protein: 11 grams, Carbohydrates: 45 grams, Fat: 9 grams, Saturated Fat: 1 grams, Cholesterol: 0 milligrams, Sodium: 577 milligrams, Fiber: 14 grams, and Sugar: 7 grams.

VEGAN SPINACH AND MUSHROOM QUICHE

A savory quiche filled with spinach, mushrooms, and tofu instead of eggs.

- Prep time: 15 minutes
- Cook time: 45 minutes
- Total time: 1 hour
- Servings: 6

Ingredients:

- 1 vegan pie crust
- 1 tablespoon olive oil
- 1/2 onion, chopped
- 2 cloves garlic, minced
- 8 oz mushrooms, sliced
- 4 oz baby spinach
- 1/2 cup vegan milk
- 1/2 cup vegan sour cream
- 1/4 cup nutritional yeast
- 1 tablespoon cornstarch
- 1/2 teaspoon salt
- 1/4 teaspoon black pepper

Directions:

1. Preheat the oven to 350°F.
2. Using a skillet over medium heat, heat up olive oil, then proceed to sauté chopped onion for 2-3 minutes until it softens. After this, add garlic and keep cooking for an additional 1-2 minutes.
3. Add the sliced mushrooms and baby spinach and cook for 5-7 minutes until the vegetables are softened and the spinach is wilted.
4. In a mixing bowl, combine the vegan milk, vegan sour cream, nutritional yeast, cornstarch, salt, and pepper. Whisk until well combined and smooth.
5. Transfer the sautéed vegetables into the bowl and mix well to ensure that they are evenly coated with the mixture.
6. Pour the mixture into the vegan pie crust and smooth the top.
7. Bake the quiche in the preheated oven for 40-45 minutes until the center is set and the crust is golden brown.

8. Take out the quiche from the oven and allow it to cool for a while before cutting and serving it.

Nutritional breakdown per serving (based on 6 servings):

Calories: 229 kcal, Protein: 7 grams, Carbohydrates: 21 grams, Fat: 12 grams, Saturated Fat: 3 grams, Cholesterol: 0 milligrams, Sodium: 223 milligrams, Fiber: 2 grams, and Sugar: 2 grams.

VEGAN BEET AND CHICKPEA BURGER

A flavorful burger made with beets, chickpeas, and spices.

- Prep time: 20 minutes
- Cook time: 20 minutes
- Total time: 40 minutes
- Servings: 4

Ingredients:

- A can (15 oz) of chickpeas, drained and rinsed
- 1 medium beet, roasted and grated
- 1/4 cup chopped onion
- 2 cloves garlic, minced
- 1/2 teaspoon ground cumin
- 1/2 teaspoon smoked paprika
- Salt and pepper, to taste
- 1/2 cup cooked quinoa
- 1/4 cup breadcrumbs
- 1 tablespoon chopped fresh parsley
- 4 whole-grain burger buns
- Toppings (lettuce, tomato, avocado, etc.)

Directions:

1. Preheat the oven to 400°F. Wrap the beet in aluminum foil and roast for 45-50 minutes until tender. Once cooled, remove the skin and grate the beet using a box grater or food processor.
2. Take a large mixing bowl and add chickpeas, grated beet, chopped onion, minced garlic, ground cumin, smoked paprika, salt, and pepper. Partially mash the mixture using a fork or potato masher, leaving some chunky bits.
3. Add the cooked quinoa, breadcrumbs, and chopped parsley to the bowl and stir until well combined.
4. Form the mixture into 4 patties.
5. Heat a non-stick skillet over medium heat. Put the patties in the frying pan and cook each side for around 5-7 minutes until they are golden brown and thoroughly heated.
6. To assemble the burger, toast the bun (if desired) and layer the patty with desired toppings (lettuce, tomato, avocado, etc.).
7. Serve immediately and enjoy!

Nutritional breakdown per serving (based on 4 servings):

Calories: 299 kcal, Protein: 14 grams, Carbohydrates: 54 grams, Fat: 5 grams, Saturated Fat: 1 grams, Cholesterol: 0 milligrams, Sodium: 357 milligrams, Fiber: 14 grams, and Sugar: 6 grams.

VEGAN PESTO PASTA SALAD

A refreshing pasta salad made with homemade pesto and fresh vegetables.

- Prep time: 15 minutes
- Cook time: 10 minutes
- Total time: 25 minutes
- Servings: 6-8

Ingredients:

- 12 oz. rotini pasta (can use chickpea rotini for higher protein)
- 1/2 cup vegan pesto
- 1 pint cherry tomatoes, halved
- 1 small cucumber, peeled, seeded, and chopped
- 1/2 red onion, finely chopped
- 1/2 cup black olives, halved
- 1/4 cup pine nuts
- Salt and pepper, to taste

Directions:

1. Take a large pot and fill it with salted water. Heat the pot over high flame until the water starts boiling.
2. Add the pasta to the boiling water and let it cook for approx. 8-10 minutes. Check to ensure it's tender, but still, have some firmness left. Drain the pasta and wash it in cold water..
3. Take a big mixing bowl and mix cooked pasta, vegan pesto, cherry tomatoes, chopped cucumber, finely chopped red onion, and halved black olives. Stir the ingredients gently until they are thoroughly combined.
4. Add salt and pepper to taste.
5. Take a dry skillet and add pine nuts to it. Heat the skillet over medium flame. Cook for 3-4 minutes, stirring frequently, until golden brown and fragrant.
6. Put the toasted pine nuts in the pasta salad and mix the ingredients together.
7. You can enjoy the pasta salad by serving it chilled or at room temperature.

Nutritional breakdown per serving (based on 6 servings):

Calories: 356 kcal, Protein: 12 grams, Carbohydrates: 44 grams, Fat: 17 grams, Saturated Fat: 2 grams, Cholesterol: 0 milligrams, Sodium: 263 milligrams, Fiber: 6 grams, and Sugar: 5 grams.

CHAPTER 3 : DINNER

MEXICAN RICE BOWL WITH BLACK BEANS

- Preparation Time: 10 minutes
- Cooking Time: 25 minutes
- Total Time: 35 minutes
- Servings: 4

Ingredients:

- 1 cup of uncooked brown rice
- 1 can black beans, drained and rinsed
- 1 small red onion, diced
- 1 small red bell pepper, diced
- 1 small yellow bell pepper, diced
- 1/4 cup of chopped cilantro
- 2 cloves of garlic, minced
- 1 tablespoon of olive oil
- 1/2 teaspoon of ground cumin
- 1/4 teaspoon of smoked paprika
- Salt and pepper, to taste
- Lime wedges, for serving (optional)

Directions:

1. Prepare the brown rice following the instructions on the package.
2. In a broad frying pan set over medium heat, warm olive oil.
3. Put garlic and red onion into the frying pan and cook until they become soft, roughly for 3-4 minutes.
4. Incorporate the chopped red and yellow bell peppers into the skillet and sauté them until they become both soft and tender, for about 5 minutes.
5. Incorporate the rinsed and drained black beans, cumin, smoked paprika, salt, and pepper to the frying pan. Mix everything thoroughly and cook until the beans are heated through, which would take approximately 2-3 minutes.
6. To assemble the bowl, divide the cooked brown rice among 4 bowls.
7. Spoon the black bean and pepper mixture over the rice in each bowl.
8. Decorate the dish with chopped cilantro and lime wedges, if desired.
9. Serve hot and enjoy!

Nutritional breakdown per serving:

Calories: 283 kcal, Protein: 11 grams, Carbohydrates: 50 grams, Fat: 5 grams, Saturated Fat: 3 grams, Sodium: 13 milligrams, Fiber: 13 grams, and Sugar: 4 grams.

LENTIL SHEPHERD'S PIE

A hearty and savory pie made with lentil filling and topped with mashed sweet potatoes or regular potatoes.

- Prep time: 20 minutes
- Cook time: 45 minutes
- Total time: 1 hour 5 minutes
- Servings: 6-8

Ingredients:

- 2 cups lentils, rinsed and drained
- 4 cups vegetable broth
- 1 tablespoon olive oil
- 1 onion, diced
- 2 garlic cloves, minced
- 2 carrots, chopped
- 2 celery stalks, chopped
- 1/4 teaspoon dried thyme
- 1/4 teaspoon dried rosemary
- Salt and pepper, to taste
- 4 cups mashed potatoes
- 1/4 cup vegan butter
- 1/4 cup unsweetened almond milk

Directions:

1. Preheat the oven to 375°F.
2. Take a large saucepan, and put in the lentils and vegetable broth. After the mixture reaches boiling point, reduce the heat and let it simmer for about 20-25 minutes until the lentils reach a soft texture, without getting too mushy. Remove any additional liquid, and keep the lentils aside.
3. Heat up a large skillet over medium heat, then pour some olive oil and warm it. Add the garlic, onions, celery, and carrots to the skillet and stir-fry the vegetables for roughly 5-7 minutes until they become tender and soft.f
4. Add the cooked lentils, thyme, rosemary, salt, and pepper to the skillet. Mix the ingredients well and let them cook together for approximately 3-4 minutes to allow their flavors to meld and blend.

5. Transfer the lentil mixture to a 9x13 inch baking dish. Evenly distribute the mashed potatoes on top of the lentils.
6. Put the dish in the oven and bake it for about 20-25 minutes until the potatoes turn a golden brown shade, and the filling gets heated through.
7. While the pie is baking, whisk together the vegan butter and almond milk in a small bowl.
8. Remove the pie from the oven and drizzle the butter mixture over the top of the potatoes.
9. Serve hot and enjoy!

Nutritional breakdown per serving (based on 8 servings):

Calories: 305 kcal, Protein: 10 grams, Carbohydrates: 46 grams, Fat: 9 grams, Saturated Fat: 3 grams, Cholesterol: 0 milligrams, Sodium: 484 milligrams, Fiber: 11 grams, and Sugar: 6 grams.

VEGAN CHILI

A protein-packed chili made with beans, lentils, and flavorful spices.

- Prep time: 15 minutes
- Cook time: 35 minutes
- Total time: 50 minutes
- Servings: 6

Ingredients:

- 1 tablespoon olive oil
- 1 onion, diced
- 2 garlic cloves, minced
- 1 red bell pepper, diced
- 1 tablespoon chili powder
- 1 teaspoon cumin
- 1/2 teaspoon smoked paprika
- 1/4 teaspoon cayenne pepper
- 1 can (28 oz) crushed tomatoes
- 1 can (15 oz) kidney beans, rinsed and drained
- Canned black beans, 15 oz, rinsed and drained
- 1 can (15 oz) corn, drained
- Salt and pepper, to taste
- Optional toppings: avocado, cilantro, lime wedges, vegan cheese

Directions:

1. In a sizeable Dutch oven/pot, add some olive oil, and preheat it at medium temperature. After that, put in the garlic and onion. Cook for approximately 3-4 minutes, until the onion starts to become translucent.
2. Add the diced bell peppers, chili powder, cumin, smoked paprika, and cayenne pepper to the pot. Mix well and cook for 2-3 minutes until the smell of the spices emanates.
3. Add the crushed tomatoes, kidney beans, black beans, corn, salt, and pepper to the pot. Mix well and allow the ingredients to reach a simmer.
4. Reduce the heat to low and let the chili simmer for 25-30 minutes, stirring occasionally, until the flavors have melded together and the vegetables are tender.
5. Add your preferred toppings, serve the meal hot, and relish it!

Nutritional breakdown per serving (based on 6 servings):

Calories: 239 kcal, Protein: 12 grams, Carbohydrates: 44 grams, Fat: 4 grams, Saturated Fat: 0.5 grams, Cholesterol: 0 milligrams, Sodium: 753 milligrams, Fiber: 13 grams, and Sugar: 10 grams.

VEGAN LENTIL CHILI

A hearty chili made with lentils and flavorful spices.

- Prep time: 15 minutes
- Cook time: 40 minutes
- Total time: 55 minutes
- Servings: 6-8

Ingredients:

- 1 tablespoon olive oil
- 1 onion, diced
- 2 garlic cloves, minced
- 1 red bell pepper, diced
- 1 green bell pepper, diced
- 1 tablespoon chili powder
- 1 teaspoon ground cumin
- 1/2 teaspoon smoked paprika
- 1/4 teaspoon cayenne pepper
- 1 can (28 oz) crushed tomatoes
- 3 cups vegetable broth
- 1 cup brown lentils, washed and drained
- 1 can (15 oz) kidney beans, rinsed and drained
- 1 can (15 oz) corn, drained
- 1 teaspoon salt
- Optional toppings: avocado, cilantro, lime wedges, vegan cheese, tortilla chips

Directions:

1. Heat up some olive oil in a large pot or Dutch oven over medium heat. Then, add garlic and onion and cook them over medium heat for around 3 to 4 minutes or until the onions become translucent.
2. Add the diced bell peppers, chili powder, cumin, smoked paprika, and cayenne pepper to the pot. Mix the ingredients well and keep cooking them for another 2-3 minutes until the aromatic properties of the spices are fully released.
3. Add the crushed tomatoes, vegetable broth, lentils, kidney beans, corn, and salt to the pot. Thoroughly mix the ingredients and bring the mixture to a boiling point.

4. Turn down the heat to the lowest possible setting and let the chili cook at a gentle simmer for approximately 30-35 minutes, stirring occasionally until the veggies reach the desired level of tenderness and the lentils are equally soft.
5. Add your preferred toppings to the dish and savor it while it's still hot!

Nutritional breakdown per serving (based on 8 servings):

Calories: 217 kcal, Protein: 13 grams, Carbohydrates: 38 grams, Fat: 3 grams, Saturated Fat: 0 grams, Cholesterol: 0 milligrams, Sodium: 660 milligrams, Fiber: 14 grams, and Sugar: 7 grams.

VEGAN TOFU STIR FRY

A stir fry with tofu, veggies, and a savory sauce.

- Prep time: 15 minutes
- Cook time: 15 minutes
- Total time: 30 minutes
- Servings: 4

Ingredients:

- Cube 14 oz of pressed extra firm tofu
- 2 tablespoons cornstarch
- 1 tablespoon sesame oil
- 1 red bell pepper, sliced
- 1 yellow bell pepper, sliced
- 1 small onion, sliced
- 2 garlic cloves, minced
- 1 tablespoon grated ginger
- 2 tablespoons soy sauce
- 1 tablespoon maple syrup
- 1 tablespoon rice vinegar
- 1 blend tablespoon of cornstarch with 1 tablespoon of cold water
- Optional toppings: sesame seeds, green onions, cilantro

Directions:

1. Take a big bowl, put in cubed tofu and 2 tablespoons of cornstarch, then mix until the tofu is coated completely.
2. Add sesame oil to a big skillet and heat it on medium-high heat. Next, add the cubed tofu to the skillet and let it cook for roughly 4-5 minutes. Ensure to periodically stir the tofu to ensure uniform cooking and achieve a crispy and golden-brown texture on all sides.
3. Take out the tofu from the skillet and keep it aside.
4. Incorporate sliced bell peppers and onions into the skillet that was previously used for tofu, and cook them for 3-4 minutes, or until they've slightly softened.
5. Introduce minced garlic and grated ginger to the skillet and mix them well. Cook for 1-2 minutes, until the fragrance of garlic and ginger emanates.

6. Take a small bowl and unite soy sauce, maple syrup, and rice vinegar. After that, pour the mixed sauce into the skillet and mix it well to ensure the vegetables are fully coated.
7. Return the cooked tofu to the skillet and mix it well along with the vegetables and sauce.
8. Add the cornstarch mixture to the skillet, then stir it well to thicken the sauce.
9. After adding your favorite toppings, serve the dish hot and enjoy!

Nutritional breakdown per serving (based on 4 servings):

Calories: 242 kcal, Protein: 15 grams, Carbohydrates: 23 grams, Fat: 11 grams, Saturated Fat: 1 grams, Cholesterol: 0 milligrams, Sodium: 652 milligrams, Fiber: 3 grams, and Sugar: 8 grams.

VEGAN SWEET POTATO AND LENTIL CURRY

A comforting curry made with sweet potatoes, lentils, and flavorful spices.

- Prep time: 10 minutes
- Cook time: 40 minutes
- Total time: 50 minutes
- Servings: 4

Ingredients:

- 1 tablespoon coconut oil
- 1 onion, chopped
- 2 garlic cloves, minced
- 2 tablespoons grated ginger
- 2 small cubes of sweet potatoes, peeled
- 1 cup red lentils, rinsed and drained
- 1 can (14 oz) diced tomatoes
- 1 can (14 oz) coconut milk
- 2 cups vegetable broth
- 2 teaspoons curry powder
- 1 teaspoon ground cumin
- 1 teaspoon ground coriander
- Salt and pepper, to taste
- Optional toppings: cilantro, chopped nuts, yogurt (or vegan yogurt), toasted coconut flakes.

Directions:

1. Warm up some coconut oil in a pot on medium heat. Sauté onion until it becomes soft for about 5 minutes. Then add garlic and ginger and cook briefly until they become fragrant.
2. Place the sweet potatoes into the pot and stir gently. Add a pinch of salt and pepper. Cook for approximately 10 minutes while stirring frequently until the sweet potatoes become slightly softened.
3. Add the lentils, diced tomatoes, coconut milk, vegetable broth, curry powder, cumin, coriander, salt, and pepper to the pot. Stir to combine.
4. Reduce the heat once the mixture boils and allow it to simmer for about 20-25 minutes. Stir occasionally, until the lentils and sweet potatoes are fully cooked and the curry has thickened to your liking.

5. Serve hot with your favorite toppings and enjoy!

Nutritional breakdown per serving (based on 4 servings):

Calories: 420 kcal, Protein: 15 grams, Carbohydrates: 59 grams, Fat: 17 grams, Saturated Fat: 13 grams, Cholesterol: 0 milligrams, Sodium: 669 milligrams, Fiber: 17 grams, and Sugar: 12 grams.

VEGAN CHICKPEA AND VEGETABLE STEW

A hearty stew with chickpeas, veggies, and a tomato-based broth.

- Prep time: 15 minutes
- Cook time: 45 minutes
- Total time: 1 hour
- Servings: 4

Ingredients:

- 2 tablespoons olive oil
- 1 onion, chopped
- 3 garlic cloves, minced
- 2 celery stalks, chopped
- 2 carrots, peeled and chopped
- 1 red bell pepper, chopped
- 2 teaspoons ground cumin
- 1 teaspoon smoked paprika
- 1/2 teaspoon ground cinnamon
- 1/4 teaspoon cayenne pepper
- Salt and pepper, to taste
- 1 can (14 oz) diced tomatoes
- 4 cups vegetable broth
- 2 cans (14 oz) chickpeas, rinsed and drained
- 2 cups chopped kale leaves
- Optional toppings: chopped parsley, lemon wedges, crusty bread

Directions:

1. Warm up the olive oil in a big pot on medium heat. Add the onion, garlic, celery, and carrots. Cook for 5-7 minutes, until the veggies are somewhat tender.
2. Add the red bell pepper, ground cumin, smoked paprika, cinnamon, cayenne pepper, salt, and black pepper to the pot. Mix well and continue cooking for an extra 5-7 minutes until the vegetables are entirely soft, and the spices release their aroma.
3. Add the diced tomatoes, vegetable broth, and chickpeas to the pot. Mix thoroughly and bring the mixture to a boil.
4. Reduce the heat to low and let the stew simmer for about 20-25 minutes. Stir occasionally, until the chickpeas are tender and the stew has thickened to your liking.

5. Mix the chopped kale into the pot and combine it well. Cook for an additional 3-5 minutes, until the kale has wilted.
6. Add your preferred toppings and savor while hot!

Nutritional breakdown per serving (based on 4 servings):

Calories: 347 kcal, Protein: 15 grams, Carbohydrates: 52 grams, Fat: 10 grams, Saturated Fat: 1 grams, Cholesterol: 0 milligrams, Sodium: 1348 milligrams, Fiber: 16 grams, and Sugar: 13 grams.

VEGAN SPAGHETTI AND MEATBALLS

A classic Italian dish with vegan meatballs made from beans, grains, and veggies, served over spaghetti.

- Prep time: 15 minutes
- Cook time: 25 minutes
- Total time: 40 minutes
- Servings: 4

Ingredients:

- 1 pound spaghetti
- 1 tablespoon olive oil
- 1 onion, chopped
- 2 cloves garlic, minced
- 1 teaspoon dried basil
- 1/2 teaspoon dried oregano
- 1/2 teaspoon salt
- 1/4 teaspoon ground black pepper
- 1/2 cup breadcrumbs
- 1/2 cup of a milk alternative like oat milk
- 1 tablespoon tomato paste
- 14 oz can of chickpeas, with the liquid drained and rinsed off
- 1/4 cup chopped parsley
- Optional toppings: vegan parmesan cheese, more chopped parsley

Directions:

1. Prepare the spaghetti as per the instructions given on the package until it is ready to be served but still firm. Strain and keep aside.
2. Using a large skillet, heat olive oil at medium to high heat. Include the onions and garlic, heat until they are softened for approximately 5 to 7 minutes while stirring regularly.
3. Incorporate the dried basil, dried oregano, salt, and black pepper into the skillet, and stir until well combined. Cook for an additional minute.
4. Combine the non-dairy milk, breadcrumbs, nutritional yeast, and tomato paste together until they are fully mixed in a separate bowl.
5. Place the chickpeas into the frying pan and then crush them to a somewhat chunky, but thoroughly pureed consistency, using a potato masher or a fork.

6. Incorporate the mixture of breadcrumbs into the frying pan and keep stirring until it is well-blended. Carry on cooking for roughly 5 minutes or until the mixture has thickened, and its sticky consistency has gone.
7. Shape the mixture into small balls, about 1-2 inches in diameter. Place the meatballs in the frying pan and cook for 5-7 minutes, flipping them occasionally, until they have a golden-brown color on all sides, and are entirely cooked inside.
8. Top the spaghetti with the meatballs and chopped parsley before serving. Add vegan parmesan cheese and more chopped parsley as desired.

Nutritional breakdown per serving (based on 4 servings):

Calories: 542 kcal, Protein: 10 grams, Carbohydrates: 95 grams, Fat: 9 grams, Saturated Fat: 1 grams, Cholesterol: 0 milligrams, Sodium: 717 milligrams, Fiber: 17 grams, and Sugar: 5 grams.

VEGAN QUINOA AND VEGETABLE STIR FRY

A flavorful stir fry with quinoa, veggies, and a homemade stir fry sauce.

- Prep time: 10 minutes
- Cook time: 20 minutes
- Total time: 30 minutes
- Servings: 4

Ingredients:

- 1 cup uncooked quinoa
- 2 cups water
- 1 tablespoon olive oil
- 1 onion, chopped
- 2 cloves garlic, minced
- 1 red bell pepper, chopped
- 1 yellow squash, sliced
- 1 zucchini, sliced
- 1 cup frozen edamame, thawed
- 2 tablespoons soy sauce
- 1 tablespoon rice vinegar
- 1 teaspoon sesame oil
- 1/4 teaspoon red pepper flakes
- Optional toppings: chopped green onions, sesame seeds

Directions:

1. Using a mesh strainer, rinse the quinoa before adding it into a medium-sized saucepan along with two cups of water. Once the mixture has boiled, lower the heat and let it simmer for around 15-20 minutes until the quinoa fully absorbs the water and becomes tender. Using a fork, fluff the quinoa before setting it aside for later use.
2. While the quinoa is cooking, put a large skillet on medium-high heat and pour olive oil into it. Allow the oil to warm up before introducing the onion and garlic to the skillet. Continue cooking the ingredients for about 3-5 minutes or until they soften.
3. Into the skillet, add the red bell pepper, yellow squash, and zucchini and mix them together using a stir. Cook for another 5-7 minutes, stirring occasionally.
4. Add the edamame to the skillet and stir to combine.
5. In a small bowl, use a whisk to blend together soy sauce, rice vinegar, sesame oil, and red pepper flakes.

6. Coat and mix the vegetables in the skillet with the sauce by pouring it over them. Cook for another 1-2 minutes, until heated through.
7. If preferred, garnish the cooked quinoa and vegetable stir-fry with chopped green onions and sesame seeds before serving.

Nutritional breakdown per serving (based on 4 servings):

Calories: 290 kcal, Protein: 12 grams, Carbohydrates: 42 grams, Fat: 8 grams, Saturated Fat: 1 grams, Cholesterol: 0 milligrams, Sodium: 532 milligrams, Fiber: 9 grams, and Sugar: 7 grams.

VEGAN SHEPHERD'S PIE

A savory pie made with lentils and topped with mashed potatoes.

- Prep time: 20 minutes
- Cook time: 50 minutes
- Total time: 1 hour and 10 minutes
- Servings: 6

Ingredients:

- 1 medium onion, diced
- 2 garlic cloves, minced
- 3 medium carrots, sliced
- 3 large potatoes, peeled and cubed for boiling
- 1/2 cup unsweetened almond milk
- 2 cups cooked brown or green lentils
- 1 cup frozen peas
- 1/2 cup frozen corn
- 1 tablespoon tomato paste
- 1 tablespoon soy sauce
- 2 tablespoons olive oil
- Salt and black pepper to taste

Directions:

1. To begin the cooking process, heat up the oven to 400°F (200°C).
2. Boil the potatoes in a large pot of salted water until tender, about 15-20 minutes. Drain and mash with almond milk until smooth, set aside.
3. Using a separate pan, sauté the onions and garlic in olive oil until the onions become translucent, generally in about 5-7 minutes. After that, include the sliced carrots and cook for an additional 5-7 minutes, or until the carrots become tender.
4. Add the cooked lentils, peas, corn, tomato paste, and soy sauce to the pan with the sautéed vegetables. Mix well and cook for another 5-7 minutes.
5. Evenly spread the mixture of lentils in a baking dish of 9x13 inches. Put the mashed potatoes on top using a spoon, and ensure the mixture is covered uniformly.
6. Bake for 25-30 minutes, or until the top is lightly browned.
7. Serve hot and enjoy!

Nutritional breakdown per serving (based on 6 servings):

Calories: 293 kcal, Protein: 12 grams, Carbohydrates: 47 grams, Fat: 7 grams, Saturated Fat: 1 grams, Cholesterol: 0 milligrams, Sodium: 206 milligrams, Fiber: 14 grams, and Sugar: 7 grams.

VEGAN SLOPPY JOES

A fun and messy meal made with lentils or tofu, tomato sauce, and spices, served on a whole wheat bun.

- Prep time: 10 minutes
- Cook time: 20 minutes
- Total time: 30 minutes
- Servings: 6

Ingredients:

- 1 tablespoon olive oil
- 1 medium onion, diced
- 1 green bell pepper, diced
- 2 cloves garlic, minced
- 1 can (15 oz) tomato sauce
- 2 tablespoons tomato paste
- 2 tablespoons brown sugar
- 1 tablespoon apple cider vinegar
- 1 tablespoon soy sauce
- 1/2 teaspoon smoked paprika
- 1/4 teaspoon cayenne pepper
- Salt and black pepper, to taste
- 1 package (12 oz) vegan crumbles
- 6 whole wheat hamburger buns

Directions:

1. Using a large skillet, heat some olive oil over medium-high heat. Add onion and green bell pepper to the skillet and cook for 5-7 minutes until they are softened.
2. Put garlic into the skillet and sauté for an additional minute.
3. Add the tomato sauce, tomato paste, brown sugar, apple cider vinegar, soy sauce, smoked paprika, cayenne pepper, salt, and black pepper to the skillet. Stir well to combine.
4. Add the vegan crumbles to the skillet and stir to coat with the sauce. Cook for 7-10 minutes, or until the sauce has thickened and the crumbles are heated through.
5. Serve the sloppy joe mixture on whole wheat hamburger buns and enjoy!

Nutritional breakdown per serving (based on 6 servings):

Calories: 250 kcal, Protein: 11 grams, Carbohydrates: 38 grams, Fat: 6 grams, Saturated Fat: 1 grams, Cholesterol: 0 milligrams, Sodium: 600 milligrams, Fiber: 7 grams, and Sugar: 14 grams.

VEGAN BLACK BEAN TACOS

A taco filled with black beans, spices, and fresh veggies.

- Prep time: 10 minutes
- Cook time: 10 minutes
- Total time: 20 minutes
- Servings: 4

Ingredients:

- 15 oz black beans, drained and washed
- 1/4 cup vegetable broth
- 1 tablespoon olive oil
- 1 teaspoon chili powder
- 1/2 teaspoon ground cumin
- 1/2 teaspoon garlic powder
- Salt and black pepper, to taste
- 8 corn tortillas
- 1 avocado, diced
- 1/4 cup chopped fresh cilantro
- 1 lime, cut into wedges

Directions:

1. In a medium saucepan, combine black beans, vegetable broth, olive oil, chili powder, cumin, garlic powder, salt, and black pepper. Simmer until the beans are heated through and the mixture thickens slightly, usually taking 5 to 7 minutes.
2. Warm the corn tortillas according to package instructions.
3. Assemble tacos by spooning the black bean mixture onto each tortilla, then adding diced avocado and chopped cilantro. Right before serving, add a lime wedge on each taco and squeeze it.

Nutritional breakdown per serving (based on 4 servings):

Calories: 233 kcal, Protein: 8 grams, Carbohydrates: 33 grams, Fat: 9 grams, Saturated Fat: 1 grams, Cholesterol: 0 milligrams, Sodium: 174 milligrams, Fiber: 10 grams, and Sugar: 1 grams.

VEGAN ZUCCHINI LASAGNA

A lighter version of lasagna made with layers of zucchini, tofu ricotta, tomato sauce, and vegan cheese.

- Prep time: 35 minutes
- Cook time: 1 hour 35 minutes
- Total time: 2 hours 10 minutes
- Servings: 8

Ingredients:

- 3 medium-sized zucchinis, sliced lengthwise
- 2 teaspoons of salt
- 1 tablespoon of olive oil
- 1 onion, chopped
- 3 cloves of garlic, minced
- 2 cups of tomato sauce
- 1 tablespoon of dried basil
- 1 tablespoon of dried oregano
- Salt and black pepper, to taste
- 1/2 cup of raw cashews
- 1/4 cup of nutritional yeast
- 1 tablespoon of lemon juice
- 1/2 teaspoon of garlic powder
- 12 lasagna noodles

Directions:

1. Slice the zucchinis lengthwise, sprinkle with salt, and let them sit for about 15 minutes to remove some of the water. After 15 minutes, rinse the slices and pat them dry with a paper towel.
2. To prepare for cooking, heat your oven to 375°F (190°C).
3. To start, warm up the olive oil using a larger skillet over medium heat. Place the garlic and onion in the skillet, and cook them for around 5 minutes until they are softened.
4. Add the tomato sauce, dried basil, dried oregano, salt, and black pepper to the skillet. Simmer for 10 minutes.
5. In a blender, blend together the raw cashews, nutritional yeast, lemon juice, garlic powder, and 1/2 cup of water until smooth.

6. Assemble the lasagna in a 9x13 inch baking dish: spoon a layer of tomato sauce on the bottom of the dish, then layer lasagna noodles, zucchini slices, tomato sauce, and cashew cheese. Repeat layers until all ingredients are used up, finishing with a layer of cashew cheese on top.
7. Place a foil over the dish and bake it for 45 minutes. Then, uncover the dish and bake for an extra 20-25 minutes or until the top turns golden brown and begins to bubble.
8. Let the lasagna cool for a few minutes before serving.

Nutritional breakdown per serving (based on 8 servings):

Calories: 279 kcal, Protein: 7 grams, Carbohydrates: 44 grams, Fat: 7 grams, Saturated Fat: 1 grams, Cholesterol: 0 milligrams, Sodium: 626 milligrams, Fiber: 77 grams, and Sugar: 5 grams.

VEGAN STUFFED SHELLS

Pasta shells stuffed with vegan ricotta cheese and veggies, topped with tomato sauce and plant-based cheese.

- Prep time: 20 minutes
- Cook time: 25 minutes
- Total time: 45 minutes
- Servings: 6 (3 shells per serving)

Ingredients:

- 18 jumbo pasta shells
- 1/2 cup raw cashews 1, soaked for at least 2 hours
- 1/2 cup unsweetened almond milk
- 1 tablespoon nutritional yeast
- 1 tablespoon lemon juice
- 1/2 teaspoon garlic powder
- Salt and pepper, to taste
- 1 tablespoon olive oil
- 1/2 medium onion, chopped
- 2 garlic cloves, minced
- 10 oz frozen spinach, squeezed dry after thawing
- 24 oz marinara sauce

Directions:

1. To begin the baking process, heat the oven to 375°F (190°C).
2. Cook the jumbo pasta shells in a pot of large salted water until it becomes al dente or as per the instructions provided in the package. Drain and rinse with cold water.
3. Using a blender, combine the soaked and drained cashews, unsweetened almond milk, nutritional yeast, lemon juice, garlic powder, salt, and pepper, then blend until it becomes a smooth mixture. Set aside.
4. Take a large skillet and keep it on medium heat, add olive oil into it. Then put onion and garlic into the skillet and cook until they become soft.
5. Add the thawed and squeezed dry spinach to the skillet, and cook for about 3 minutes or until heated through.
6. Combine the spinach mixture with the cashew 'ricotta' mixture.
7. Apply a layer of marinara sauce on the bottom of a baking dish which is 9x13 inches in size.

8. Fill each pasta shell with a mixture of spinach and cashews, then put the stuffed shells into the baking dish.
9. Apply the leftover marinara sauce on top of the shells.
10. To begin, cover the dish with aluminum foil, place it in the oven, and bake for 20 minutes. Then, remove the dish from the oven, take the foil off, and continue baking for an additional 5 minutes until the top of the dish is lightly browned and bubbly.
11. Let the stuffed shells cool for a few minutes before serving.

Nutritional breakdown per serving (based on 6 servings):

Calories: 322 kcal, Protein: 10 grams, Carbohydrates: 46 grams, Fat: 11 grams, Saturated Fat: 1 grams, Cholesterol: 0 milligrams, Sodium: 350 milligrams, Fiber: 5 grams, and Sugar: 9 grams.

CHICKPEA CURRY

A delicious and comforting curry made with chickpeas and a flavorful curry sauce.

- Prep time: 10 minutes
- Cook time: 25 minutes
- Total time: 35 minutes
- Servings: 4

Ingredients:

- 2 tablespoons oil
- 1 medium onion, finely chopped
- 1 tablespoon ginger garlic paste
- 2 to 3 green chilies, slit
- 4 medium tomatoes, finely chopped or pureed
- 1 teaspoon salt, or to taste
- 1 teaspoon cumin powder
- 1 teaspoon coriander powder
- 1/2 teaspoon turmeric powder
- 1/2 teaspoon red chili powder
- 1/2 teaspoon garam masala powder
- 2 cups cooked chickpeas (or 1 can of chickpeas, drained and rinsed)
- 1/2 cup water
- Cilantro leaves, chopped, for garnish

Directions:

1. Heat oil in a pan on medium heat.
2. Add onions and sauté until they turn golden brown.
3. Add ginger-garlic paste and green chilies, and sauté for a minute.
4. Add tomatoes, salt, and all the spices, and sauté for 6-7 minutes, or until the oil separates from the sides.
5. Add chickpeas and water. Mix well and bring to a boil.
6. Reduce heat to low and let it simmer for 10-15 minutes, or until the gravy thickens and the chickpeas are well coated with the spices.
7. Add some cilantro leaves as a garnish and serve hot, with either rice or bread.

Nutritional breakdown per serving (based on 4 servings):

Calories: 238 kcal, Protein: 8 grams, Carbohydrates: 30 grams, Fat: 10 grams, Saturated Fat: 1 grams, Cholesterol: 0 milligrams, Sodium: 652 milligrams, Fiber: 9 grams, and Sugar: 7 grams.

VEGAN BOLOGNESE

A hearty and satisfying pasta sauce made with lentils, veggies, and tomato sauce.

- Prep time: 15 minutes (plus soaking time)
- Cook time: 35 minutes Total time: 50 minutes
- Servings: 4

Ingredients:

- 1 cup dried green lentils, soaked overnight and rinsed
- 1 tablespoon olive oil
- 1 onion, chopped
- 2 garlic cloves, minced
- 1 large carrot, chopped
- 1 celery stalk, chopped
- 1 (14.5 ounce) can crushed tomatoes
- 1/2 cup vegetable broth
- 1 teaspoon dried oregano
- 1/2 teaspoon dried basil
- Salt and pepper, to taste
- 8 ounces pasta of your choice (spaghetti or fusilli work well)
- Chopped fresh parsley, for garnish (optional)

Directions:

1. In a large pot, add the soaked and rinsed lentils and enough water to cover them by about one inch. Bring to a boil, then reduce heat to low and let simmer for about 20-25 minutes, or until tender. Drain and set aside.
2. To begin, heat olive oil in a sizeable skillet using medium heat. After that, add the onion and garlic to the skillet and cook them until they have softened.
3. Add carrot and celery to the skillet, and cook for about 5 minutes, or until they are tender.
4. Add crushed tomatoes, vegetable broth, oregano, basil, salt, and pepper to the skillet. Bring to a boil.
5. Lower the heat to a minimal and add the cooked lentils. Let them simmer for around 10 to 15 minutes.
6. While the lentil mix is simmering, cook pasta according to package directions. Drain and set aside.
7. Serve the lentil Bolognese over the pasta. Garnish with chopped parsley, if desired.

Nutritional breakdown per serving (based on 4 servings):

Calories: 375 kcal, Protein: 20 grams, Carbohydrates: 67 grams, Fat: 5 grams, Saturated Fat: 1 grams, Cholesterol: 0 milligrams, Sodium: 316 milligrams, Fiber: 16 grams, and Sugar: 10 grams.

SWEET POTATO AND BLACK BEAN ENCHILADAS

Enchiladas filled with sweet potato, black beans, and flavorful spices, topped with avocado and vegan sour cream.

- Prep time: 15 minutes
- Cook time: 45 minutes
- Total time: 60 minutes
- Servings: 4-6

Ingredients:

- 2 small sweet potatoes, diced
- 1 tablespoon olive oil
- 1 medium onion, chopped
- 3 garlic cloves, minced
- 15-oz can of black beans, washed
- 1 teaspoon ground cumin
- 1/2 teaspoon chili powder
- Salt and pepper, to taste
- 8-10 corn tortillas
- 2 cups shredded cheese of your choice
- 1 (16-ounce) jar of salsa
- Chopped fresh cilantro, for garnish

Directions:

1. Preheat the oven to 375°F.
2. Put the sweet potatoes in a spacious pot, add water until they are covered, and bring it to a boiling point. Cook until they are tender, about 10-12 minutes. Drain and set aside.
3. Warm up the olive oil in a big skillet on medium heat. Put in the onions and garlic and continue cooking until they become soft.
4. Add the black beans, cumin, chili powder, salt, and pepper to the skillet. Add the cooked sweet potatoes and mix well.
5. Pour approximately 1/3 of the salsa into the base of a 9x13 inch baking dish.
6. Warm the tortillas according to package instructions. Spoon the sweet potato and black bean mixture onto each tortilla. Roll up and place seam-side down in the baking dish.

7. After that, pour the remaining salsa over the enchiladas and sprinkle shredded cheese on top.
8. Bake for around 25 to 30 minutes, or until the cheese is melted properly and the enchiladas are heated through.
9. Garnish with fresh cilantro and serve hot.

Nutritional breakdown per serving (based on 6 servings):

Calories: 520 kcal, Protein: 21 grams, Carbohydrates: 58 grams, Fat: 22 grams, Saturated Fat: 6 grams, Cholesterol: 0 milligrams, Sodium: 1190 milligrams, Fiber: 9 grams, and Sugar: 11 grams.

VEGAN SHEPHERD'S PIE WITH LENTILS AND MUSHROOMS

Another version of the hearty shepherd's pie made with lentils, mushrooms, veggies, and topped with mashed potatoes.

- Prep time: 20 minutes
- Cook time: 50 minutes
- Total time: 70 minutes
- Servings: 6-8

Ingredients:

- 2 tablespoons olive oil
- 1 onion, diced
- 2 garlic cloves, minced
- 2 cups sliced mushrooms
- 2 cups cooked green lentils
- 1 cup frozen peas
- 1 cup frozen corn
- 1 cup vegetable broth
- 2 tablespoons tomato paste
- 1 teaspoon dried thyme
- Salt and pepper, to taste
- 4-5 large potatoes, peeled and chopped
- 1/2 cup unsweetened plant-based milk
- 2 tablespoons vegan butter

Directions:

1. Heat the oven to 375°F before starting the cooking process.
2. Using a big skillet, heat olive oil over medium heat. Once heated, put in onion and garlic and cook until both are softened.
3. Include mushrooms in the skillet and cook them for approximately 5-7 minutes until they release their liquid and get brown.
4. Add cooked lentils, peas, corn, vegetable broth, tomato paste, thyme, salt, and pepper to the skillet. Warm up the mix until it simmers, then let it cook for about 10-15 minutes until the sauce thickens and the vegetables become tender.

5. As the lentil mixture cooks, take a large pot, add chopped potatoes, and cover them completely with cold water. Warm up the blend until it comes to a boil on high heat. Then, reduce the heat to medium-low and let it simmer for 15-20 minutes until the potatoes turn soft and tender.
6. Remove the water from the pot containing potatoes and place them back in the same pot. Add plant-based milk and vegan butter, and mash until smooth and creamy.
7. Transfer the lentil mixture to a large baking dish. Smooth the mashed potatoes over the top.
8. Bake for 25-30 minutes, or until the potatoes are browned and the filling is heated through.
9. Let cool for a few minutes before serving.

Nutritional breakdown per serving (based on 8 servings):

Calories: 267 kcal, Protein: 10 grams, Carbohydrates: 46 grams, Fat: 6 grams, Saturated Fat: 1 grams, Cholesterol: 0 milligrams, Sodium: 269 milligrams, Fiber: 12 grams, and Sugar: 5 grams.

VEGAN BUFFALO CAULIFLOWER WRAPS

A spicy and tangy wrap made with cauliflower, buffalo sauce, and veggies.

- Prep Time: 10 minutes
- Cook Time: 25 minutes
- Total Time: 35 minutes
- Servings: 4

Ingredients: For the Buffalo Cauliflower:

- 1 medium cauliflower, cut into small pieces
- 1 cup all-purpose flour
- 1 cup unsweetened plant-based milk
- 1 teaspoon garlic powder
- 1 teaspoon smoked paprika
- 1/2 teaspoon salt
- 1/4 teaspoon black pepper
- 3/4 cup buffalo hot sauce
- Cooking spray

For the Wraps:

- 4 large wraps or tortillas
- 1 cup shredded carrots
- 1 cup shredded cabbage
- 4 green onions, sliced
- 1/4 cup ranch dressing (vegan, if desired)

Directions:

1. Preheat oven to 450°F.
2. In a large bowl mix together flour, plant-based milk, garlic powder, smoked paprika, salt, and pepper.
3. Add cauliflower florets to the mix and stir until they're coated.
4. Take the cauliflower coated in the mixture and spread it evenly on a baking sheet covered with parchment paper, then apply a coat of cooking spray.
5. Place in the oven preheated to the desired temperature and bake for 20 minutes, turning halfway through.
6. Remove from oven and place buffalo sauce over cauliflower florets.

7. Bake for additional 5 minutes until the florets look crispy.
8. Spread 1 tablespoon of ranch dressing (vegan, if desired) over each wrap.
9. Divide the buffalo cauliflower, shredded cabbage, shredded carrots and sliced green onions among the 4 wraps.
10. Roll up each wrap, tucking in the sides as you go. Serve warm.

Nutritional breakdown per serving:

Calories: 369 kcal, Protein: 11 grams, Carbohydrates: 63 grams, Fat: 9 grams, Saturated Fat: 2 grams, Cholesterol: 0 milligrams, Sodium: 2483 milligrams, Fiber: 7 grams, and Sugar: 9 grams.

VEGAN PECAN AND CRANBERRY STUFFED SQUASH

Vegan Pecan and Cranberry Stuffed Squash is a delicious and healthy dish that features tender and flavorful roasted squash stuffed with a savory mix of pecans and cranberries. This recipe is both vegan-friendly and simple to prepare, making it an ideal dish for any event or gathering.

- Preparation Time: 15 minutes
- Cooking Time: 1 hour 30 minutes
- Total Time: 1 hour 45 minutes
- Servings: 4

Ingredients:

- 2 acorn squashes, halved and seeds removed
- 1 tablespoon of olive oil
- 1 small yellow onion, diced
- 2 cloves of garlic, minced
- 1 cup of cooked brown rice
- 1/2 cup of chopped pecans, plus extra for topping
- 1/2 cup of dried cranberries
- 1 teaspoon of dried thyme
- Salt and pepper, to taste
- Fresh parsley, for serving (optional)

Directions:

1. Before starting the cooking process, preheat the oven to 375°F/190°C.
2. Arrange the acorn squash halves evenly in a spacious baking dish and leave it aside.
3. Next, heat the olive oil on medium-high heat in a large skillet.
4. Afterwards, add the diced onion and garlic to the skillet and sauté for approximately 3-4 minutes until they become soft.
5. Add the cooked brown rice, chopped pecans, dried cranberries, dried thyme, salt, and pepper to the skillet. Stir well to combine.
6. Spoon the rice mixture into each of the squash halves, packing it in tightly.
7. After you have covered the baking dish using aluminum foil, carefully put it in the oven for about 1 hour and 15 minutes to bake. It is done when the acorn squash turns tender and can be effortlessly pierced by a fork.

8. Remove the foil and sprinkle additional chopped pecans over the top of each squash half.
9. Resume baking the squash for an additional 10 to 15 minutes or until the pecans become toasted and turn a light brown color.
10. As soon as you remove the dish from the oven, serve it while it's still piping hot. If you like, you may add a sprinkle of freshly chopped parsley on top of the dish to give it a decorative touch.

Nutritional breakdown per serving:

Calories: 345 kcal, Protein: 7 grams, Carbohydrates: 54 grams, Fat: 14 grams, Saturated Fat: 6 grams, Sodium: 160 milligrams, Fiber: 8 grams, and Sugar: 17 grams.

VEGAN CHICKPEA MEATLOAF WITH MUSHROOM GRAVY

Vegan Chickpea Meatloaf with Mushroom Gravy is a tasty and satisfying plant-based version of a classic comfort food. This savory loaf is made with chickpeas, vegetables, and herbs, and is smothered in a rich and flavorful mushroom gravy. This dish is perfect for a hearty and healthy meal that everyone will love.

- Preparation Time: 15 minutes
- Cooking Time: 1 hour
- Total Time: 1 hour 15 minutes
- Servings: 4-6

Ingredients:

For the Chickpea Meatloaf:

- 2 cans of chickpeas, drained and rinsed
- 1 small onion, finely chopped
- 2 cloves garlic, minced
- 1/2 cup of rolled oats
- 1/2 cup of tomato sauce
- 1 tablespoon of olive oil
- 1 tablespoon of soy sauce
- 1 tablespoon of nutritional yeast
- 1 teaspoon of dried basil
- 1 teaspoon of dried oregano
- 1/2 teaspoon of salt
- Black pepper, to taste

For the Mushroom Gravy:

- 2 tablespoons of olive oil
- 1 small onion, finely chopped
- 2 cloves garlic, minced
- 8 oz of mushrooms, sliced
- 2 tablespoons of all-purpose flour
- 2 cups of vegetable broth

- 1 teaspoon of soy sauce
- Black pepper, to taste

Directions:

1. Ensure to set the oven temperature to 375°F/190°C and wait for it to preheat before starting to cook.
2. Using a food processor, blend together the chickpeas, onion, garlic, rolled oats, tomato sauce, olive oil, soy sauce, nutritional yeast, basil, oregano, salt, and black pepper until they are well combined. Avoid overblending and aim for a coarse, not pureed, texture.
3. After greasing a loaf pan, transfer the mixture into it and use a spatula to spread and level the top surface evenly.
4. Bake the chickpea meatloaf in the preheated oven for 40-45 minutes or until golden brown.
5. While the chickpea meatloaf is baking, prepare the mushroom gravy.
6. Place a large saucepan over medium heat and pour the olive oil to heat it up.
7. Add the chopped onion and garlic and sauté until softened, about 3-4 minutes.
8. Place the sliced mushrooms into the heated pan and sauté for approximately 5-6 minutes, or until they become tender and develop a golden-brown color.
9. Evenly distribute and blend the flour mixture onto the mushrooms by sprinkling it over the top, and then stir it thoroughly to ensure that both ingredients are well combined.
10. Pour the vegetable broth slowly into the saucepan, while continuously whisking it to avoid the formation of lumps.
11. Adjust the seasoning of the dish to your preference by adding soy sauce and black pepper as per your taste.
12. Reduce the heat to low and let the gravy simmer for 10-15 minutes, stirring occasionally, until it thickens.
13. When the chickpea meatloaf is finished baking, let it cool for a few minutes before slicing it.
14. Serve the sliced chickpea meatloaf with the mushroom gravy on top. Enjoy!

Nutritional breakdown per serving (based on 6 servings):

Calories: 247 kcal, Protein: 10 grams, Carbohydrates: 67 grams, Fat: 8 grams, Saturated Fat: 1 grams, Sodium: 880 milligrams, Fiber: 14 grams, and Sugar: 0 grams.

VEGAN ROASTED VEGETABLE PASTA

A flavorful pasta dish with roasted veggies, garlic, and olive oil.

- Prep Time: 15 minutes
- Cook Time: 25 minutes
- Total Time: 40 minutes
- Servings: 4

Ingredients:

- 1 medium zucchini, diced
- 1 medium yellow squash, diced
- 1 red bell pepper, diced
- 1 yellow bell pepper, diced
- 1 small red onion, diced
- 3 garlic cloves, minced
- 2 tablespoons olive oil
- Salt and pepper, to taste
- 8 ounces whole wheat pasta
- 1/4 cup chopped fresh basil
- 1/4 cup chopped fresh parsley

Directions:

1. Preheat oven to 400°F.
2. Evenly coat the diced vegetables and minced garlic with 2 tablespoons of olive oil by tossing them in a large bowl.
3. Cover the baking sheet with parchment paper, distribute the vegetables uniformly and add salt and pepper to season according to your personal taste. Allow the vegetables to bake for a period of 20-25 minutes, or until they become tender and acquire a golden-brown color.
4. While the vegetables are baking, fill a large pot with water, add salt to it and put it on the stove to heat. Allow water to boil and then cook the pasta in it for about 8-10 minutes till it reaches an al dente consistency. Drain the pasta and set it aside for the next step. Drain and set aside.
5. Take a big bowl and mix the roasted vegetables and cooked pasta in it. Top with chopped fresh basil and parsley.
6. Serve hot and enjoy!

Nutritional breakdown per serving:

Calories: 300 kcal, Protein: 11 grams, Carbohydrates: 45 grams, Fat: 10 grams, Saturated Fat: 1 grams, Cholesterol: 0 milligrams, Sodium: 50 milligrams, Fiber: 9 grams, and Sugar: 0 grams.

VEGAN SESAME TOFU BOWLS

A bowl with crispy tofu, sesame seeds, and fresh veggies, served over brown rice.

- Prep Time: 15 minutes
- Cook Time: 25 minutes
- Total Time: 40 minutes
- Servings: 4

Ingredients:

- 14 ounces extra-firm tofu, drained and pressed
- 1 tablespoon cornstarch
- 1/2 teaspoon salt
- 1/4 teaspoon black pepper
- 2 tablespoons sesame oil
- 4 garlic cloves, minced
- 1 tablespoon grated ginger
- 1/4 cup tamari or soy sauce
- 1/4 cup rice vinegar
- 2 tablespoons maple syrup
- 1 tablespoon cornstarch
- 4 cups cooked brown rice
- 4 cups mixed vegetables (such as broccoli, bell pepper, and carrots)
- 2 tablespoons sesame seeds
- Fresh basil or cilantro, for garnish (optional)

Directions:

1. Preheat oven to 400°F.
2. Cut the pressed tofu into small cubes and place them in a mixing bowl. Put 1 tablespoon of cornstarch, 0.5 teaspoon of salt, and 0.25 teaspoon of black pepper into the bowl mentioned above. Thoroughly mix all the ingredients until well combined.
3. Take a large skillet and heat 1 tablespoon of sesame oil on medium heat. Add the tofu cubes and cook for around 10 to 15 minutes, flipping them occasionally, until the cubes are crispy and golden brown in color.
4. Take another bowl and whisk together the minced garlic, grated ginger, tamari or soy sauce, rice vinegar, maple syrup, and 1 tablespoon cornstarch until it turns smooth.

5. Add the mixed vegetables to the skillet with the tofu and sauté for 5-7 minutes, until they're tender-crisp.
6. Pour the sauce over the vegetables and tofu, stirring until the sauce has thickened and coated the tofu and vegetables.
7. Divide the cooked brown rice among four bowls. Top with the tofu and vegetable mixture, sprinkle with sesame seeds, and garnish with fresh basil or cilantro if desired.
8. Serve hot and enjoy!

Nutritional breakdown per serving: Calories:

475 kcal, Protein: 22 grams, Carbohydrates: 67 grams, Fat: 15 grams, Saturated Fat: 2 grams, Cholesterol: 0 milligrams, Sodium: 1100 milligrams, Fiber: 10 grams, and Sugar: 0 grams.

VEGAN LENTIL SLOPPY JOES

Vegan Lentil Sloppy Joes are a tasty and healthy twist on the classic comfort food. The dish features tender lentils simmered in a tangy tomato sauce, piled onto buns for a hearty vegan meal. If you're in the mood for a satisfying and simple plant-based meal, this recipe is perfect for you!

- Preparation Time: 15 minutes
- Cooking Time: 30 minutes
- Total Time: 45 minutes
- Servings: 6

Ingredients:

- 1 cup dry lentils, rinsed and drained
- 4 cups of vegetable broth
- 1 small onion, diced
- 1 green bell pepper, diced
- 1 can (14.5 oz) diced tomatoes
- 1/2 cup of tomato sauce
- 1 tablespoon of olive oil
- 1 tablespoon of chili powder
- 1 tablespoon of brown sugar
- 1/2 tablespoon of cumin
- 1/2 teaspoon of smoked paprika
- 1/4 teaspoon of salt
- Black pepper, to taste
- 6 whole wheat hamburger buns, toasted

Directions:

1. Add lentils and vegetable broth to a saucepan of medium size. Increase the heat, and let the mixture come to a boil before reducing the heat to allow it to simmer for 20-25 minutes, until the lentils are fully cooked and tender.
2. On medium heat, warm the olive oil up in a large skillet.
3. Sauté the diced green pepper and onion in the skillet for around 5-7 minutes, or until they have softened.
4. Add the diced tomatoes, tomato sauce, cooked lentils, chili powder, brown sugar, cumin, smoked paprika, salt, and black pepper to the skillet. Stir well to combine.

5. Lower the heat to a minimum and let the mixture simmer for an extra 10-15 minutes, with occasional stirring to allow the flavors to combine and the mixture to slightly thicken.

6. When the consistency of the sloppy joe mixture is to your preference, take it off the heat and serve it over whole wheat hamburger buns that have been toasted.

Nutritional breakdown per serving:

Calories: 254 kcal, Protein: 13 grams, Carbohydrates: 67 grams, Fat: 3 grams, Saturated Fat: 0 grams, Sodium: 601 milligrams, Fiber: 15 grams, and Sugar: 0 grams.

VEGAN BROCCOLI AND TOFU STIR FRY

A stir-fry loaded with broccoli, tofu, and a homemade ginger sauce.

- Prep Time: 15 minutes
- Cook Time: 10 minutes
- Total Time: 25 minutes
- Servings: 4

Ingredients:

- 14 ounces extra-firm tofu, drained and pressed
- 2 tablespoons soy sauce
- 1 tablespoon cornstarch
- 2 tablespoons sesame oil
- Broccoli, small and chopped
- 1 red bell pepper, seeded and chopped
- 2 garlic cloves, minced
- 1/2 teaspoon grated ginger
- 2 tablespoons vegetable broth
- Salt and pepper, to taste
- Cooked brown rice, for serving

Directions:

1. Cut the pressed tofu into small cubes and place them in a bowl with the soy sauce and cornstarch. Toss to coat.
2. Heat a large skillet at medium-high temperature and add 1 tablespoon of sesame oil subsequently. Add the tofu cubes and cook for 5-7 minutes, until crispy and golden brown. Remove from the skillet and set aside on a plate.
3. In the same skillet, heat another tablespoon of sesame oil over medium-high heat. Add the broccoli florets, chopped red bell pepper, minced garlic, and grated ginger. Stir-fry for 3-4 minutes, until the vegetables are tender-crisp.
4. Add the cooked tofu to the skillet with the vegetables, along with 2 tablespoons of vegetable broth. Stir-fry for an additional 1-2 minutes, until everything is heated through.
5. Season with salt and pepper to taste. Serve hot over cooked brown rice.

Nutritional breakdown per serving:

Calories: 262 kcal, Protein: 15 grams, Carbohydrates: 3 grams, Fat: 18 grams, Saturated Fat: 2 grams, Cholesterol: 0 milligrams, Sodium: 644 milligrams, Fiber: 4 grams, and Sugar: 0 grams.

VEGAN CREAMY MUSHROOM PASTA

A creamy pasta dish with mushrooms, onions, and garlic.

- Prep Time: 10 minutes
- Cook Time: 20 minutes
- Total Time: 30 minutes
- Servings: 4

Ingredients:

- 12 ounces whole wheat or gluten-free pasta
- 2 tablespoons olive oil
- 1 small onion, finely chopped
- 4 garlic cloves, minced
- 1/2 teaspoon dried thyme
- 16 ounces mushrooms, sliced
- 1 cup vegetable broth
- Soak 1/2 cup of cashews for 2 hours or overnight
- 1/4 cup nutritional yeast
- 1 tablespoon lemon juice
- Salt and pepper, to taste
- Fresh parsley, chopped, for serving

Directions:

1. In a large pot of boiling water with salt, cook the pasta for 8-10 minutes until it becomes al dente. Drain the pasta and keep it aside.
2. Heat the olive oil in a large skillet over medium heat. Then, add onion and cook until it is translucent for about 2-3 minutes. Following this, pour in the garlic and thyme and cook for an additional minute.
3. Put the sliced mushrooms in the skillet and cook for 6-7 minutes, mixing occasionally till they turn tender and lightly brown.
4. Using a blender, combine vegetable broth, soaked cashews, nutritional yeast, and lemon juice, blending until a smooth and creamy consistency is achieved.
5. Pour the sauce over the mushrooms in the skillet and bring to a simmer, stirring consistently, for approximately 5 minutes until the sauce thickens.
6. Put the cooked pasta in the skillet containing the sauce and mushrooms. Mix everything well until the pasta is evenly coated with the sauce and heated thoroughly.
7. Season with salt and pepper to taste. Serve hot, topped with fresh parsley.

Nutritional breakdown per serving:

Calories: 451 kcal, Protein: 16 grams, Carbohydrates: 57 grams, Fat: 20 grams, Saturated Fat: 3 grams, Cholesterol: 0 milligrams, Sodium: 122 milligrams, Fiber: 9 grams, and Sugar: 0 grams.

VEGAN QUINOA CHILI

A protein-packed chili made with quinoa and flavored with spices and veggies.

- Prep Time: 20 minutes
- Cook Time: 45 minutes
- Total Time: 1 hour 5 minutes
- Servings: 6

Ingredients:

- 1 tablespoon olive oil
- 1 onion, chopped
- 1 green bell pepper, chopped
- 1 red bell pepper, chopped
- 3 garlic cloves, minced
- 1 tablespoon chili powder
- 1 teaspoon ground cumin
- 1/2 teaspoon smoked paprika
- 1/4 teaspoon cayenne pepper
- 28 ounce can crushed tomatoes
- Drained and rinsed 15 oz kidney beans
- Drained and rinsed 15 oz black beans
- 1 cup quinoa, rinsed
- 2 cups vegetable broth
- Salt and pepper, to taste

Directions:

1. In a large pot, heat olive oil on medium heat. Include the bell peppers and onion and cook until the onion turns translucent.
2. Put in the minced garlic, and sauté for an additional minute.
3. Add the chili powder, cumin, smoked paprika, and cayenne pepper, and stir until fragrant.
4. Add the crushed tomatoes, kidney beans, black beans, quinoa, and vegetable broth to the pot, and stir to combine.
5. Simmer the mixture and then lower the heat to low and cover it with a lid. Leave the chili to cook at a low simmer for about 35-40 minutes, occasionally stirring, until the quinoa turns tender, and the flavors blend together nicely.

6. Sprinkle salt and pepper onto the dish based on your preference and serve it quickly while it's still hot.

Nutritional breakdown per serving:

Calories: 309 kcal, Protein: 17 grams, Carbohydrates: 56 grams, Fat: 5 grams, Saturated Fat: 1 grams, Cholesterol: 0 milligrams, Sodium: 710 milligrams, Fiber: 16 grams, and Sugar: 0 grams.

VEGAN GREEK MOUSSAKA

A Greek dish made with lentils, eggplant, and a creamy béchamel sauce, topped with vegan cheese.

- Prep Time: 30 minutes
- Cook Time: 1 hour
- Total Time: 1 hour 30 minutes
- Servings: 8

Ingredients: For the eggplant layer:

- 3 large eggplants, sliced lengthwise into 1/4 inch slices
- 1 tablespoon olive oil
- Salt and pepper, to taste

For the lentil filling:

- 1 tablespoon olive oil
- 1 large onion, chopped
- 3 garlic cloves, minced
- 1 cup lentils, washed and drained
- 2 cups vegetable broth
- 14.5 ounce can diced tomatoes
- 1 tablespoon tomato paste
- 1/2 teaspoon ground cinnamon
- 1/4 teaspoon ground nutmeg
- Salt and pepper, to taste

For the potato layer:

- 3 large potatoes, peeled and sliced thinly

For the bechamel sauce:

- 3 tablespoons vegan butter
- 3 tablespoons all-purpose flour
- 2 cups unsweetened almond milk

- 1/4 teaspoon ground nutmeg

- Salt and pepper, to taste

Directions:

1. Preheat your oven to 350°F.

2. Firstly, place a large frying pan over medium heat. Include approximately one tablespoon of olive oil with it. After that, add diced onion and minced garlic and keep stirring until they soften.

3. Add in the tomato paste, chopped tomatoes, oregano, basil, salt, and pepper. Stir and bring to a boil.

4. Lower the heat and allow it to simmer for an additional 10 minutes.

5. Add in the drained and rinsed lentils and stir well. Simmer for another 5 minutes or until the lentils have absorbed the flavors of the bolognese. Set aside.

6. Using a different pan, warm 1 tablespoon of olive oil over medium heat. Add the sliced eggplant and potatoes to the pan and sprinkle with salt and pepper. Cook for 5 minutes on each side or until they are golden brown. Set aside.

7. For preparing vegan béchamel sauce, warm 2 tablespoons of olive oil in a saucepan on medium heat. Add the all-purpose flour and whisk until it forms a roux.

8. Gradually add the unsweetened almond milk, whisking constantly to avoid lumps. Simmer the sauce until it thickens up.

9. Customize the salt and pepper seasoning of the sauce to suit your taste.

Nutritional breakdown per serving:

Calories: 345 kcal, Protein: 11 grams, Carbohydrates: 39 grams, Fat: 17 grams, Saturated Fat: 2 grams, Cholesterol: 0 milligrams, Sodium: 830 milligrams, Fiber: 11 grams, and Sugar: 8 grams.

VEGAN LASAGNA

Layered lasagna sheets with tofu ricotta, veggies, and a homemade tomato sauce.

- Prep Time: 30 minutes
- Cook Time: 1 hour
- Total Time: 1 hour 30 minutes
- Servings: 6

Ingredients

- 1 tablespoon olive oil
- 1 large onion, chopped
- 4 cloves garlic, minced
- 8 oz mushrooms, sliced
- 2 teaspoons dried oregano
- 2 teaspoons dried basil
- 1 teaspoon salt
- 1/4 teaspoon black pepper
- 1 (28 oz) can crushed tomatoes
- 1 (15 oz) can tomato sauce
- 1 (6 oz) can tomato paste
- 2 tablespoons sugar
- 12 lasagna noodles
- 4 cups vegan mozzarella cheese
- 1/2 cup shredded vegan parmesan cheese
- Fresh basil leaves for garnish (optional)

Directions

1. Heat the oven to 375°F. Apply cooking spray on a baking dish that measures 9x13 inches.
2. Warm up some olive oil in a spacious skillet at a moderate heat. Add onion and garlic, and sauté for 3-4 minutes until softened.
3. Add mushrooms, oregano, basil, salt, and black pepper and continue to sauté until the mushrooms release their water and become slightly browned.
4. Add crushed tomatoes, tomato sauce, tomato paste, and sugar. Stir well and reduce heat to low. Simmer for 20-25 minutes.
5. Cook lasagna noodles according to package directions. Drain and set aside.
6. On the base of the baking dish previously prepared, layer 1/3 of the tomato sauce.

7. Arrange 4 cooked lasagna noodles over the sauce.
8. Spread another 1/3 of the tomato sauce over the noodles.
9. Sprinkle with 1 cup of vegan mozzarella cheese.
10. Repeat the layers of noodles, tomato sauce, and cheese 2 more times, ending with a layer of tomato sauce on top.
11. Sprinkle with vegan parmesan cheese.
12. Put it in the oven for around 30-35 minutes or until the cheese has melted and is frothy.
13. Let the lasagna cool for 10 minutes and afterward cut it into pieces. Top the pieces with fresh basil leaves as a garnish.

Nutritional breakdown per serving:

Calories: 374 kcal, Protein: 0 grams, Carbohydrates: 26 grams, Fat: 12 grams, Saturated Fat: 8 grams, Cholesterol: 0 milligrams, Sodium: 370 milligrams, Fiber: 7 grams, and Sugar: 10 grams.

VEGAN SUSHI BOWLS

A fun and colorful bowl with sushi rice, veggies, and tofu

- Prep time: 15 minutes
- Cook time: 30 minutes
- Total time: 45 minutes
- Servings: 4

Ingredients:

- 2 cups short-grain brown rice
- 2 cups water
- 1/4 cup rice vinegar
- 2 tbsp maple syrup
- 1/2 tsp salt
- 1 large carrot, peeled and grated
- 1 small cucumber, sliced
- 1 avocado, sliced
- 1/4 cup pickled ginger
- 1/4 cup chopped scallions
- 2 tbsp toasted sesame seeds

For the dressing:

- 1/4 cup soy sauce
- 1 tbsp rice vinegar
- 1 tbsp maple syrup
- 1 tsp grated ginger
- 1 tsp sesame oil

Directions:

1. Wash the brown rice under cold water until the water turns transparent.
2. In a medium saucepan, pour the cleaned rice and water. Put the pan on high flame and heat the water until it reaches boiling point. After that, reduce the heat to low and cover the pan with a lid. Give the rice around 30 minutes to cook or until it has become soft and absorbed all the water.

3. Combine the rice vinegar, maple syrup, and salt in a small bowl and whisk them together. Drizzle the mixture onto the already cooked rice and mix well to combine all the ingredients. Divide the cooked rice evenly among four bowls.
4. Top each bowl with grated carrot, sliced cucumber, sliced avocado, pickled ginger, chopped scallions, and toasted sesame seeds.
5. Take a small bowl to blend soy sauce, rice vinegar, maple syrup, grated ginger and sesame oil, by whisking them together. Once the dressing is ready, dribble it over each bowl and serve.

Nutritional breakdown per serving:

Calories: 410 kcal, Protein: 11 grams, Carbohydrates: 65 grams, Fat: 15 grams, Saturated Fat: 2 grams, Cholesterol: 0 milligrams, Sodium: 1402 milligrams, Fiber: 11 grams, and Sugar: 13 grams.

CHAPTER 4 : DESSERTS

VEGAN CHOCOLATE CHIP COOKIES

A classic cookie recipe made with plant-based butter and vegan chocolate chips.

- Prep time: 15 minutes
- Cook time: 12-15 minutes
- Total time: 27-30 minutes
- Servings: 24 cookies

Ingredients:

- 2 cups all-purpose flour
- 1 tsp baking powder
- 1/2 tsp salt
- 1 cup vegan butter, softened
- 3/4 cup brown sugar
- 3/4 cup white sugar
- 1/4 cup unsweetened applesauce
- 1 tsp vanilla extract
- 1 cup vegan chocolate chips

Directions:

1. Preheat the oven to 350°F. Line a baking sheet with parchment paper.
2. Using a mixing bowl, combine the flour, baking powder, and salt, then whisk them together.
3. Take another bowl and with the help of an electric mixer, beat the vegan butter, brown sugar, and white sugar together until it lightens in color and becomes fluffy.
4. Add the unsweetened applesauce and vanilla extract to the butter mixture. Mix until well combined.
5. Blend the wet ingredients with the flour mixture slowly and regularly, ensuring they are uniformly mixed. Avoid overmixing and stop mixing once the two are comparatively combined.
6. Stir in the vegan chocolate chips.
7. Prepare a baking sheet and, using a rounded tablespoonful of cookie dough, drop the dough onto the sheet, making sure to space the cookies 2-3 inches apart.
8. Put the cookies in the oven and bake them for approximately 12 to 15 minutes, or until the edges have turned a light golden brown color and the centers are firm.
9. Immediately after baking, allow the cookies to rest for two minutes on the baking sheet before transferring them to a wire rack for thorough cooling.

Nutritional breakdown per serving:

Calories: 160 kcal, Protein: 1 grams, Carbohydrates: 21 grams, Fat: 8 grams, Saturated Fat: 3 grams, Cholesterol: 0 milligrams, Sodium: 120 milligrams, Fiber: 1 grams, and Sugar: 12 grams.

VEGAN BANANA BREAD

A comforting bread made with mashed ripe bananas, flour, and cinnamon.

- Prep time: 10 minutes
- Cook time: 50-60 minutes
- Total time: 1 hour 10 minutes
- Servings: 12

Ingredients:

- 3 ripe bananas, mashed
- 1/3 cup vegetable oil
- 1/2 cup brown sugar
- 1 tsp vanilla extract
- 1 1/2 cups all-purpose flour
- 1 tsp baking soda
- 1/2 tsp salt
- 1/2 tsp ground cinnamon
- 1/4 tsp ground nutmeg

Directions:

1. Preheat the oven to 350°F. Grease a 9x5-inch loaf pan.
2. In a bowl for mixing, blend the mashed bananas, vegetable oil, brown sugar and vanilla extract together.
3. Mix the flour, baking soda, salt, cinnamon, and nutmeg in another bowl using a whisk.
4. Move the mixture to the loaf pan that has been prepared.
5. Transfer the mixture to the loaf pan that has been prepared.
6. Place the mixture into the oven and bake it for 50-60 minutes. After that, check if it's done by inserting a toothpick at the center of the bread. If there's no batter sticking to the toothpick, then the bread is ready.
7. Wait for 5 minutes while letting the banana bread cool in the pan. After that, transfer it to a wire rack and let it cool entirely.

Nutritional breakdown per serving:

Calories: 171 kcal, Protein: 2 grams, Carbohydrates: 26 grams, Fat: 7 grams, Saturated Fat: 1 grams, Cholesterol: 0 milligrams, Sodium: 220 milligrams, Fiber: 2 grams, and Sugar: 12 grams.

VEGAN STRAWBERRY NICE CREAM

A dairy-free ice cream made with frozen strawberries and coconut milk.

- Prep time: 5 minutes
- Cook time: 0 minutes
- Total time: 5 minutes
- Servings: 4

Ingredients:

- 4 cups frozen strawberries
- 1/4 cup unsweetened almond milk
- 2 Tbsp maple syrup
- 1 tsp vanilla extract

Directions:

1. Mix together frozen strawberries, almond milk, maple syrup, and vanilla extract and transfer the mixture to a blender or food processor. Process the mixture until it is smooth in texture. Process the mixture until it is smooth in texture.
2. Process until a smooth and creamy mixture is formed, while scraping down the sides as necessary.
3. If desired, transfer the nice cream to an airtight container and freeze for 30 minutes to 1 hour to firm up.
4. Scoop the nice cream into bowls or cones and serve immediately.

Nutritional breakdown per serving:

Calories: 66 kcal, Protein: 1 grams, Carbohydrates: 16 grams, Fat: 0.5 grams, Saturated Fat: 0 grams, Cholesterol: 0 milligrams, Sodium: 5 milligrams, Fiber: 3 grams, and Sugar: 11 grams.

PEANUT BUTTER BANANA OAT BARS

A hearty and filling bar recipe made with mashed bananas, peanut butter, oats, and nuts.

- Prep time: 10 minutes
- Cook time: 25 minutes
- Total time: 35 minutes
- Servings: 12 bars

Ingredients:

- 2 ripe bananas, mashed
- 1/2 cup creamy peanut butter
- 1/4 cup honey
- 2 cups old-fashioned oats
- 1 tsp vanilla extract
- 1/2 tsp ground cinnamon
- 1/4 tsp salt

Directions:

1. Preheat the oven to 350°F. Cover the base and sides of an 8x8-inch baking dish with parchment paper.
2. Take a mixing bowl and mix mashed bananas, peanut butter, and honey. Combine the components until they are fully integrated.
3. Add the oats, vanilla extract, cinnamon, and salt to the mixture. Stir until all of the ingredients are fully incorporated.
4. Empty the mixture into the baking dish that has been previously prepared and distribute it uniformly by pressing it down.
5. Put it in the oven and bake for approximately 25 minutes, or until the edges acquire a slight golden brown hue and the center is firm.
6. Allow the oat bars to cool completely in the baking dish before slicing them into 12 bars.

Nutritional breakdown per serving:

Calories: 192 kcal, Protein: 5 grams, Carbohydrates: 26 grams, Fat: 8 grams, Saturated Fat: 1 grams, Cholesterol: 0 milligrams, Sodium: 80 milligrams, Fiber: 3 grams, and Sugar: 5 grams.

VEGAN PEANUT BUTTER ENERGY BALLS

A snack made with peanut butter, oats, and maple syrup rolled into balls.

- Prep time: 10 minutes
- Cook time: 0 minutes
- Total time: 10 minutes
- Servings: 12 balls

Ingredients:

- 1 cup old-fashioned oats
- 1/2 cup creamy peanut butter
- 1/4 cup honey
- 2 Tbsp ground flaxseeds
- 1/4 tsp salt

Directions:

1. In a mixing bowl, combine the oats, peanut butter, honey, flaxseeds, and salt. Stir until all of the ingredients are fully incorporated.
2. Form the mixture into 12 balls, using your hands to roll them into shape.
3. Transfer the balls to an airtight container and refrigerate them for at least 1 hour before serving.
4. Store any remaining energy balls in the refrigerator for up to 1 week.

Nutritional breakdown per serving:

Calories (1 energy ball): 110 kcal, Protein: 4 grams, Carbohydrates: 12 grams, Fat: 6 grams, Saturated Fat: 1 grams, Cholesterol: 0 milligrams, Sodium: 55 milligrams, Fiber: 2 grams, and Sugar: 5 grams.

VEGAN BLUEBERRY MUFFINS

A sweet and fruity muffin recipe made with fresh or frozen blueberries.

- Prep time: 10 minutes
- Cook time: 20 minutes
- Total time: 30 minutes
- Servings: 12 muffins

Ingredients:

- 2 cups all-purpose flour
- 1/2 cup granulated sugar
- 2 tsp baking powder
- 1/4 tsp baking soda
- 1/4 tsp salt
- 1 cup unsweetened almond milk
- 1/4 cup coconut oil, melted
- 1 tsp vanilla extract
- 1.5 cups fresh or frozen blueberries

Directions:

1. Preheat the oven to 375°F. Get the muffin tin ready for use by either lining it with paper liners or applying a non-stick spray coating.
2. Place all-purpose flour, granulated sugar, baking powder, baking soda, and salt in a mixing bowl. Mix these dry ingredients thoroughly until they are completely combined.
3. Grab a different mixing bowl and mix together the almond milk, melted coconut oil, and vanilla extract. Stir these ingredients well until they are evenly combined.
4. Make sure not to overmix while combining the dry and wet ingredients, stir until fully incorporated.
5. Fold in 1 cup of blueberries, reserving the remaining 1/2 cup.
6. Transfer the mixture into the muffin tin that has been made ready, ensuring that each muffin cup is about two-thirds full.
7. Top each muffin cup with the reserved blueberries.
8. Put the muffin tray in the oven and bake for about 20-25 minutes or until the muffins are slightly golden-brown and when checked with a toothpick in the center, it should come out clean, indicating that the muffins are fully baked.

Nutritional breakdown per serving:

Calories (1 muffin): 158 kcal, Protein: 2 grams, Carbohydrates: 27 grams, Fat: 5 grams, Saturated Fat: 4 grams, Cholesterol: 0 milligrams, Sodium: 108 milligrams, Fiber: 1 grams, and Sugar: 11 grams.

VEGAN CHOCOLATE AVOCADO PUDDING

A creamy and chocolatey dessert made with avocados and cocoa powder.

- Prep time: 5 minutes
- Cook time: 0 minutes
- Total time: 5 minutes
- Servings: 2

Ingredients:

- 1 ripe avocado, pitted and peeled
- 1/4 cup cocoa powder
- 1/4 cup maple syrup
- 1/4 cup unsweetened almond milk
- 1 tsp vanilla extract

Directions:

1. In either a blender or a food processor, combine avocado, cocoa powder, almond milk, maple syrup, and vanilla extract together. Process until smooth.
2. Divide the pudding into two serving dishes.
3. It is suggested to keep in the refrigerator for at least 30 minutes before serving.

Nutritional breakdown per serving:

Calories (1/2 of recipe): 215 kcal, Protein: 3 grams, Carbohydrates: 30 grams, Fat: 12 grams, Saturated Fat: 4 grams, Cholesterol: 0 milligrams, Sodium: 52 milligrams, Fiber: 7 grams, and Sugar: 18 grams.

VEGAN CHOCOLATE PROTEIN BALLS

A protein-packed snack made with dates, nuts, and cocoa powder.

- Prep time: 10 minutes
- Cook time: 0 minutes
- Total time: 35 minutes
- Servings: 12 balls

Ingredients:

- 1 cup rolled oats
- 1/4 cup vegan chocolate protein powder
- 1/4 cup almond butter
- 1/4 cup maple syrup
- 1 tsp vanilla extract

Directions:

1. Combine the rolled oats and vegan chocolate protein powder in a mixing bowl and stir them well to amalgamate.
2. Add the almond butter, maple syrup, and vanilla extract to the bowl. Mix well until fully combined.
3. With the help of a cookie scoop or a spoon, create 12 balls from the mixture ensuring that they are properly shaped by rolling them between your hands.
4. After rolling the balls, place them in an airtight container and keep them in the refrigerator for a minimum of 25 minutes before serving.
5. Store any remaining protein balls in the refrigerator for up to 1 week.

Nutritional breakdown per serving:

Calories (1 ball): 98 kcal, Protein: 4 grams, Carbohydrates: 13 grams, Fat: 4 grams, Saturated Fat: 0 grams, Cholesterol: 0 milligrams, Sodium: 5 milligrams, Fiber: 2 grams, and Sugar: 5 grams.

CHOCOLATE CHIA SEED PUDDING

A creamy and rich dessert made with chia seeds, plant-based milk, and cocoa powder.

- Prep time: 5 minutes
- Cook time: 0 minutes
- Total time: 25 minutes (includes chilling time)
- Servings: 2

Ingredients:

- 1/4 cup chia seeds
- 1 cup unsweetened almond milk
- 2 tbsp cocoa powder
- 2 tbsp maple syrup
- 1/4 tsp vanilla extract

Directions:

1. Put the chia seeds, almond milk, cocoa powder, maple syrup, and vanilla extract in a mixing bowl and thoroughly combine them. Stir them thoroughly to achieve a well-mixed mixture of all the ingredients.
2. Let the mixture sit for about 5 minutes, then whisk again to further combine the ingredients.
3. After covering the bowl with plastic wrap, refrigerate it for a duration of not less than twenty minutes or until the mixture has obtained desirable thickness.
4. Once thickened, divide the pudding into two serving containers.
5. Serve the pudding chilled and enjoy!

Nutritional breakdown per serving:

Calories (1/2 of recipe): 173 kcal, Protein: 6 grams, Carbohydrates: 23 grams, Fat: 10 grams, Saturated Fat: 1 grams, Cholesterol: 0 milligrams, Sodium: 96 milligrams, Fiber: 11 grams, and Sugar: 7 grams.

HOMEMADE GRANOLA BARS

A chewy and crunchy snack made with oats, nuts, and dried fruit.

- Prep time: 10 minutes
- Cook time: 20 minutes
- Total time: 30 minutes
- Servings: 12 bars

Ingredients:

- 2 cups rolled oats
- 1/2 cup nuts (e.g. almonds, walnuts), chopped
- 1/4 cup honey
- 1/4 cup coconut oil
- 1/4 cup brown sugar
- 1 tsp vanilla extract
- 1/2 tsp cinnamon
- 1/4 tsp salt
- 1/2 cup dried fruit (e.g. raisins, cranberries), chopped

Directions:

1. To start the recipe, preheat your oven to 350°F (180°C) and line an 8x8 inch baking dish with parchment paper.
2. Mix the rolled oats and chopped nuts in a large mixing bowl.
3. Using a small saucepan, combine and melt the honey, coconut oil, and brown sugar over medium heat until fully combined for around 2-3 minutes.
4. Take the saucepan off the heat and mix in the vanilla extract, cinnamon, and salt.
5. After preparing the baking dish, transfer the mixture into it and press it down firmly. Bake the mixture for 20-25 minutes until the edges turn golden brown.
6. Add in the dried fruit and stir again to combine.
7. After pouring the mixture into the prepared baking dish, press it down firmly. Bake until the edges turn golden brown for about 20-25 minutes.
8. Bake for 20-25 minutes, or until the edges are golden brown.
9. Take the dish out of the oven and allow it to cool down completely. After that, cut it into 12 bars.
10. Keep the granola bars in a sealed container at room temperature for a maximum of 7 days.

Nutritional breakdown per serving:

Calories (1 bar): 216 kcal, Protein: 4 grams, Carbohydrates: 27 grams, Fat: 11 grams, Saturated Fat: 5 grams, Cholesterol: 0 milligrams, Sodium: 69 milligrams, Fiber: 3 grams, and Sugar: 15 grams.

VEGAN PEANUT BUTTER CHOCOLATE CHIP GRANOLA BARS

A soft granola bar made using peanut butter, oats, and vegan chocolate chips.

- Prep time: 10 minutes
- Cook time: 0 minutes (no-bake)
- Total time: 1 hour 10 minutes
- Servings: 12 bars

Ingredients:

- 2 cups rolled oats
- 1/2 cup smooth peanut butter
- 1/2 cup maple syrup
- 1/2 cup mini chocolate chips (vegan)
- 1 tsp vanilla extract

Directions:

1. Cover an 8x8 inch baking dish with parchment paper.
2. In a mixing bowl, combine the rolled oats, peanut butter, maple syrup, mini chocolate chips, and vanilla extract. Stir well to fully combine all ingredients.
3. Transfer the blend to the previously lined baking dish and press it firmly with your hands or a spatula, ensuring even distribution and compactness.
4. Refrigerate the baking dish for at least 1 hour, or until the mixture has hardened.
5. Once hardened, remove the mixture from the baking dish using the parchment paper to lift it out.
6. Cut the mixture into 12 bars using a sharp knife.
7. You can preserve the granola bars in a sealed container in a fridge for a maximum of 7 days.

Nutritional breakdown per serving:

Calories (1 bar): 234 kcal, Protein: 6 grams, Carbohydrates: 32 grams, Fat: 10 grams, Saturated Fat: 3.5 grams, Cholesterol: 0 milligrams, Sodium: 31 milligrams, Fiber: 3 grams, and Sugar: 16 grams.

VEGAN OATMEAL RAISIN COOKIES

A soft and chewy cookie recipe made with raisins and oats.

- Prep time: 15 minutes
- Cook time: 12 minutes
- Total time: 27 minutes
- Servings: 16 cookies

Ingredients:

- 1/2 cup vegan butter, softened
- 1/2 cup brown sugar
- 1/4 cup white sugar
- 1 flax egg (1 tbsp ground flaxseed + 3 tbsp water)
- 1 tsp vanilla extract
- 3/4 cup all-purpose flour
- 1/2 tsp baking soda
- 1/2 tsp cinnamon
- 1/4 tsp salt
- 1 1/2 cups rolled oats
- 1/2 cup raisins

Directions:

1. Firstly, heat your oven to 350°F (180°C) and get a baking sheet ready by covering it with parchment paper.
2. Take a mixing bowl and beat the vegan butter, brown sugar, and white sugar together until the mixture is light and fluffy.
3. Include the flax egg and vanilla extract into the mixing bowl, and stir thoroughly to combine the ingredients.
4. Take another mixing bowl and whisk together the all-purpose flour, baking soda, cinnamon, and salt.
5. Thoroughly combine the dry and wet ingredients while stirring them together fully.
6. Fold in the rolled oats and raisins.
7. Using a scoop, place onto the prepared baking sheet 2 tablespoon-sized portions of the dough with a space of 2 inches between each.
8. Bake until the edges turn golden brown, usually for about 12-15 minutes.

9. Take the baking sheet out of the oven and let the cookies cool down for 5-10 minutes before transferring them to a wire rack for complete cooling. Make sure the cookies have been cooled down completely before storing them.
10. You can keep the cookies fresh by storing them in an airtight container at room temperature for a maximum of 1 week.

Nutritional breakdown per serving:

Calories (1 cookie): 175 kcal, Protein: 3 grams, Carbohydrates: 28 grams, Fat: 6 grams, Saturated Fat: 2 grams, Cholesterol: 0 milligrams, Sodium: 111 milligrams, Fiber: 2 grams, and Sugar: 14 grams.

VEGAN APPLE CRISP

A warm and comforting dessert made with apples, oats, and cinnamon.

- Prep time: 15 minutes
- Cook time: 45 minutes
- Total time: 60 minutes
- Servings: 6

Ingredients:

- 6 medium apples, peeled and sliced
- 1/3 cup brown sugar
- 1/2 cup all-purpose flour
- 1/2 cup rolled oats
- 1/2 cup vegan butter, melted
- 1 tsp ground cinnamon
- 1/4 tsp ground nutmeg
- 1/4 tsp salt

Directions:

1. Ensure the oven is heated to 375°F (190°C) before beginning the baking process.
2. Take a mixing bowl and mix the sliced apples, brown sugar, cinnamon, nutmeg, and salt. Mix them well to ensure the apples are evenly coated.
3. Transfer the apple mixture to a 9x9 inch baking dish and spread it out evenly.
4. Combine the all-purpose flour, rolled oats, and melted vegan butter in a separate mixing bowl and mix thoroughly until well combined.
5. Spread the flour and oat mixture over the apple mixture in the baking dish, making sure to cover all of the apples evenly.
6. Put the apple crisp in the oven that has been preheated, and let it bake for 45 minutes, or until the topping obtains a golden brown color and the apples become tender.
7. Take the baking dish out of the oven and allow the apple crisp to cool for approximately 5-10 minutes before serving.
8. Serve the apple crisp warm, with vegan ice cream or whipped cream if desired.

Nutritional breakdown per serving:

Calories: 327 kcal, Protein: 2 grams, Carbohydrates: 52 grams, Fat: 13 grams, Saturated Fat: 8 grams, Cholesterol: 0 milligrams, Sodium: 197 milligrams, Fiber: 5 grams, and Sugar: 33 grams.

VEGAN PUMPKIN SPICE MUFFINS

A fall-inspired muffin recipe made with pumpkin puree and warm spices.

- Prep time: 10 minutes
- Cook time: 20 minutes
- Total time: 30 minutes
- Servings: 12 muffins

Ingredients:

- 1 1/2 cups all-purpose flour
- 1 tsp baking powder
- 1 tsp baking soda
- 1 tsp ground cinnamon
- 1/2 tsp ground ginger
- 1/2 tsp ground nutmeg
- 1/4 tsp ground cloves
- 1/4 tsp salt
- 1 cup canned pumpkin puree
- 1/2 cup coconut sugar
- 1/4 cup coconut oil, melted
- 1/4 cup almond milk
- 1 tsp vanilla extract

Directions:

1. Heat up your oven to a temperature of 350°F (180°C) before use. Cover the muffin tin with paper liners or spray with cooking spray before use.
2. Using a mixer, combine all-purpose flour, baking powder, baking soda, cinnamon, ginger, nutmeg, cloves, and salt in a large mixing bowl until well combined.
3. Mix the pumpkin puree, coconut sugar, melted coconut oil, almond milk, and vanilla extract together in a separate mixing bowl until they form a smooth mixture.
4. Mix the dry and wet ingredients together gently until they are just incorporated and blended.
5. Use a scooper to add the muffin batter into the muffin tin, making sure to fill each muffin cup about 2/3 full.
6. After the oven has been preheated, put the muffins inside and bake for 18-20 minutes, or until a toothpick inserted into the center of a muffin comes out clean.

7. Take out the muffins from the oven and leave them to cool for 5-10 minutes in the muffin tin before shifting them to a wire rack to cool completely.
8. It's possible to store the muffins for a period of 3 days at room temperature in an airtight container, or alternatively, up to 1 month in the freezer.

Nutritional breakdown per serving (1 muffin):

Calories: 124 kcal, Protein: 2 grams, Carbohydrates: 0 grams, Fat: 5 grams, Saturated Fat: 4 grams, Cholesterol: 0 milligrams, Sodium: 199 milligrams, Fiber: 2 grams, and Sugar: 7 grams.

VEGAN ALMOND BUTTER CUPS

A healthier take on peanut butter cups made with almond butter and dark chocolate.

- Prep time: 20 minutes
- Cook time: 0 minutes
- Total time: 20 minutes
- Servings: 12 cups

Ingredients:

- 1 cup vegan chocolate chips
- 1/2 cup almond butter
- 1/4 cup coconut oil, melted
- 1/4 cup maple syrup
- 1/4 tsp salt
- 1/4 cup chopped almonds (optional)

Directions:

1. Put 12 paper liners in a muffin tin.
2. In a microwave-safe dish, melt the vegan chocolate chips completely by stirring every 15 seconds.
3. Take a small quantity of melted chocolate and put it at the base of each paper liner. Use a spoon or brush to spread it up along the edges of the liner to create a chocolate shell.
4. Place the muffin tin in the freezer to set the chocolate shells while you make the almond butter filling.
5. Whisk almond butter, melted coconut oil, maple syrup, and salt together in a mixing bowl until smooth and thoroughly combined.
6. Take out the muffin tin from the freezer and put around one tablespoon of almond butter filling into each chocolate shell.
7. Cover the almond butter filling completely by spooning the leftover melted chocolate over it, and using a brush or spoon to spread it out.
8. Sprinkle chopped almonds over the top of the chocolate, if desired.
9. Return the muffin tin to the freezer to set the chocolate and almond butter filling for at least 10 minutes.
10. Once the chocolate has become firm, take out the almond butter cups from the muffin tin and place them in an airtight container in the fridge or freezer until they are ready to be served.

Nutritional breakdown per serving (1 almond butter cup):

Calories: 178 kcal, Protein: 3 grams, Carbohydrates: 13 grams, Fat: 14 grams, Saturated Fat: 7 grams, Cholesterol: 0 milligrams, Sodium: 58 milligrams, Fiber: 2 grams, and Sugar: 9 grams.

VEGAN CINNAMON SUGAR DONUTS

A sweet and fluffy donut recipe made with applesauce and whole wheat flour.

- Prep time: 15 minutes
- Cook time: 10 minutes
- Total time: 25 minutes
- Servings: 12 donuts

Ingredients: For the donuts:

- 2 cups all-purpose flour
- 2 tsp baking powder
- 1/2 tsp baking soda
- 1/4 tsp salt
- 3/4 cup almond milk
- 1/2 cup vegan butter, melted
- 1/2 cup granulated sugar
- 1 tsp vanilla extract

For the cinnamon sugar coating:

- 1/2 cup granulated sugar
- 2 tsp ground cinnamon
- 1/4 cup melted vegan butter

Directions:

1. To begin, heat up the oven to 375°F (190°C) and use cooking spray to grease a donut pan.
2. Whisk all-purpose flour, baking powder, baking soda, and salt together in a large mixing bowl until they are thoroughly combined.
3. Combine the almond milk, melted vegan butter, granulated sugar, and vanilla extract in a different mixing bowl by whisking them together until fully combined.
4. Combine the dry and wet ingredients together, stirring until they are just mixed, while being cautious not to overmix.
5. Using a spoon, add the prepared donut batter to each donut mold, filling them approximately 2/3 of the way full.
6. Once the oven is preheated, put the donuts inside it and bake for 8 to 10 minutes until a toothpick inserted into the center of a donut comes out clean.

7. After cooking, let the donuts sit in the pan for a brief period before transferring them to a wire rack to cool thoroughly.
8. Create the cinnamon sugar coating by mixing the granulated sugar and ground cinnamon in a shallow dish, then whisk the combination thoroughly.
9. Prior to rolling it in the cinnamon sugar mixture until it is fully coated, dip each donut in melted vegan butter.
10. You can either serve the cinnamon sugar donuts right away or store them in an airtight container for up to three days at room temperature.

Nutritional breakdown per serving (1 donut):

Calories: 240 kcal, Protein: 2 grams, Carbohydrates: 31 grams, Fat: 12 grams, Saturated Fat: 6 grams, Cholesterol: 0 milligrams, Sodium: 257 milligrams, Fiber: 1 grams, and Sugar: 16 grams.

VEGAN CHOCOLATE CHIA PUDDING

A creamy and rich dessert made with chia seeds, plant-based milk, and cocoa powder.

- Prep time: 10 minutes
- Cook time: 0 minutes
- Total time: 10 minutes
- Servings: 2-4

Ingredients:

- 1/4 cup chia seeds
- 1 cup almond milk
- 2 tbsp maple syrup
- 2 tbsp unsweetened cocoa powder
- 1 tsp vanilla extract
- A pinch of salt

Directions:

1. Mix the chia seeds, almond milk, maple syrup, cocoa powder, vanilla extract, and salt together until they are well combined, using a mixing bowl and a whisk.
2. Let the mixture rest for 5-10 minutes, stirring from time to time to prevent the formation of lumps.
3. Once the mixture has thickened and the chia seeds have absorbed the liquid, transfer the pudding to serving bowls or jars.
4. Refrigerate the pudding for a minimum of 30 minutes before serving, or let it sit overnight for a thicker texture.
5. Serve the chocolate chia pudding cold, topped with fresh fruit, nuts, or coconut whipped cream, if desired.

Nutritional breakdown per serving (1/2 cup):

Calories: 123 kcal, Protein: 4 grams, Carbohydrates: 17 grams, Fat: 6 grams, Saturated Fat: 1 grams, Cholesterol: 0 milligrams, Sodium: 11 milligrams, Fiber: 8 grams, and Sugar: 6 grams.

VEGAN COCONUT MACAROONS

A crunchy and chewy cookie recipe made with shredded coconut and maple syrup.

- Prep time: 10 minutes
- Cook time: 15 minutes
- Total time: 25 minutes
- Servings: 12 macaroons

Ingredients:

- 2 cups unsweetened shredded coconut
- 1/2 cup maple syrup
- 1/4 cup coconut oil, melted
- 1 tsp vanilla extract
- 1/4 tsp salt

Directions:

1. Before baking, ensure that your oven is preheated to 350°F (180°C) and cover the baking sheet with parchment paper before adding your ingredients.
2. Combine the shredded coconut, maple syrup, melted coconut oil, vanilla extract, and salt in a mixing bowl and whisk everything together until fully blended.
3. Scoop out the macaroon batter onto the baking sheet using a cookie scoop or tablespoon. Ensure to leave enough space between each scoop which should be around 2 inches to avoid them from sticking together.
4. Bake the macaroons in the preheated oven for 12-15 minutes, or until the edges are golden brown and the tops are set.
5. Once the baking time for the macaroons is complete, take them out of the oven and let them cool on the baking sheet for around 5 minutes. Then, use a wire rack to transfer them and let them cool completely. It is important not to rush the cooling process and allow the macaroons to cool entirely on the wire rack.
6. You can either serve the vegan coconut macaroons right away or keep them in a sealed container at room temperature for up to 5 days.

Nutritional breakdown per serving (1 macaroon):

Calories: 157 kcal, Protein: 1 grams, Carbohydrates: 8 grams, Fat: 14 grams, Saturated Fat: 12 grams, Cholesterol: 0 milligrams, Sodium: 30 milligrams, Fiber: 8 grams, and Sugar: 5 grams.

CHOCOLATE CHIP ZUCCHINI BREAKFAST COOKIES

A grab-and-go cookie recipe made with shredded zucchini, oats, and vegan chocolate chips.

- Prep time: 15 minutes
- Cook time: 25 minutes
- Total time: 40 minutes
- Servings: 12 cookies

Ingredients:

- 1 cup old-fashioned oats/
- 1/2 cup almond flour
- 1/4 cup unsweetened shredded coconut
- 1/4 cup coconut sugar
- 1/4 cup mini chocolate chips
- 1/2 cup grated zucchini
- 1/4 cup almond butter
- 1/4 cup maple syrup
- 1 tsp vanilla extract
- 1/2 tsp baking powder
- 1/4 tsp salt

Directions:

1. Set the oven temperature to 350°F (180°C) and get a baking tray ready by laying a sheet of parchment paper on it.
2. Combine the oats, almond flour, shredded coconut, coconut sugar, mini chocolate chips, baking powder, and salt in a mixing bowl until the mixture is evenly incorporated.
3. In a separate bowl, whisk together the grated zucchini, almond butter, maple syrup, and vanilla extract until fully combined.
4. Combine the dry and wet ingredients by pouring the latter into the former, and continue mixing until the dough is completely blended.
5. Scoop the cookie dough with a tablespoon or cookie scoop, and place the scoops on a prepared baking sheet with a gap of around 2 inches between each.
6. Flatten the cookies gently with a fork or spatula.
7. Bake the cookies in the oven that has been preheated for 22-25 minutes or until the edges become a light golden brown and the centers are set.

8. After baking, give the cookies about 5 minutes to cool on the baking sheet before shifting them to a wire rack for complete cooling.
9. Enjoy the chocolate chip zucchini breakfast cookies right after baking or store them in an airtight container at room temperature for a maximum of 5 days.

Nutritional breakdown per serving (1 cookie):

Calories: 145 kcal, Protein: 4 grams, Carbohydrates: 16 grams, Fat: 8 grams, Saturated Fat: 2 grams, Cholesterol: 0 milligrams, Sodium: 59 milligrams, Fiber: 2 grams, and Sugar: 8 grams.

MINI DARK CHOCOLATE ALMOND BUTTER CUPS

A healthier take on peanut butter cups made with almond butter and dark chocolate.

- Prep time: 30 minutes
- Cook time: 0 minutes
- Total time: 30 minutes
- Servings: 12 mini cups

Ingredients:

- 1 cup dark chocolate chips
- 1/4 cup creamy peanut butter
- 1/4 cup powdered sugar
- 1/4 tsp salt
- 1/4 tsp vanilla extract

Directions:

1. Cover a mini muffin tin with mini muffin liners and keep it aside.
2. Dissolve the dark chocolate chips in a microwave-safe dish or a double boiler. Keep stirring every half a minute until the chips dissolve completely and the mixture becomes smooth.
3. With the help of a teaspoon, put a small quantity of melted chocolate into the base of each mini muffin liner.
4. In a separate bowl, mix together the creamy peanut butter, powdered sugar, salt, and vanilla extract until fully combined and smooth.
5. Form the peanut butter mixture into tiny balls and put one ball into each mini muffin liner on the top of the layer of melted chocolate.
6. Add more melted chocolate on top of each peanut butter ball, making sure to completely cover it and fill the liner up to the top.
7. Chill the miniature peanut butter cups for a minimum of 20 minutes until the chocolate sets in the refrigerator.
8. Indulge in the mini dark chocolate peanut butter cups immediately or preserve them in an airtight container inside the fridge for a maximum of 1 week.

Nutritional breakdown per serving (1 mini peanut butter cup):

Calories: 123 kcal, Protein: 2 grams, Carbohydrates: 12 grams, Fat: 8 grams, Saturated Fat: 4 grams, Cholesterol: 0 milligrams, Sodium: 52 milligrams, Fiber: 2 grams, and Sugar: 8 grams.

CONCLUSION

The rising popularity of plant-based lifestyles can be attributed to an increasing awareness of health, sustainability, and animal welfare issues. The plant-based way of eating prioritizes whole foods, which may include fruits, vegetables, whole grains, and legumes, among others. Numerous studies have found that consuming this type of diet is associated with an array of health benefits, including a lower chance of developing chronic conditions such as diabetes and heart disease.

The Plant-Based Cookbook provides a collection of 20 snack and dessert recipes that are not just mouth-watering but also quick to make and nutritious. The recipes center around whole food ingredients and do not use animal products, making them a great option for those looking to incorporate more plant-based options into their daily routine. From Vegan Chocolate Chip Cookies to Vegan Sweet Potato Brownies, each recipe has been carefully crafted to provide a satisfying and flavorful experience.

In addition to being healthy and delicious, these recipes are designed for meal prep, making it easier for individuals to incorporate plant-based snacks and desserts into their busy schedules. By preparing snacks and desserts ahead of time, individuals can reduce the temptation to reach for unhealthy options and ensure that they have wholesome and nutritious options readily available.

The Plant-Based Cookbook provides an excellent reference for individuals who want to include more plant-based meals into their eating habits or for those who are searching for healthy and flavorful snack and dessert choices. Selecting a plant-based diet can create a positive impact on one's health, the environment, and animal welfare, which makes it a desirable lifestyle choice for many people.

Made in the USA
Las Vegas, NV
10 January 2024